TRAVELS WITH KING KONG

A Journey from the Known to the Unknown

Written by

James Henderson

Travels With King Kong

A Journey from the Known to the Unknown

by

James Henderson

This book is written to provide information and motivation to readers. It's purpose is not render any type of psychological, legal, or professional advice of any kind. The content is the sole opinion and expression of the author.

ISBN: 979-8-218-95494-9 Paperback

Printed in the United States of America.

James Henderson
PO Box 325
Redlands, CA 92373

CONTENT

PREFACE:

(How the journey began and who was John?) .... *i*

INTRODUCTION

(SIAFU Overland Expedition – What was it like?). .... *iii*

CHAPTER 1

Seattle to Tangiers (From the known to the unknown) *1*

CHAPTER 2

MOROCCO AND ALGERIA

(Encounters with exotic and strange cultures) *6*

CHAPTER 3

The Sahara Desert

(Overwhelming heat and desolation) *22*

CHAPTER 4:

Nigeria – The Cameroons – Central African Republic

(A welcome change of scenery) *43*

CHAPTER 5

Zaire and the Congo (Into deepest, darkest Africa) *65*

CHAPTER 6

East Africa (Finally on Safari). *104*

CHAPTER 7

Nairobi - Mombasa - Lamu Island

(The Big City at last, and discovery of an Island Paradise)............. 127

CHAPTER 8

Mt. Kilimanjaro (Journey to the roof of Africa) 175

CHAPTER 9

Northern Kenya (Off the beaten path) 204

CHAPTER 10

Leaving Africa – Arriving London

(Goodbye to one world – hello to another)..241

CHAPTER 11

Returning Home

(Forever changed, and with memories for a lifetime........................249

EPILOGUE

(From then to now – Changes in Africa since 1974-1975).................256

APPENDIX / ADDENDUM...258

CONTENT

PREFACE:

(How the journey began and who was John?) ....*i*

INTRODUCTION

(SIAFU Overland Expedition –What was it like?). ....*iii*

CHAPTER 1

Seattle to Tangiers (From the known to the unknown).......................*1*

CHAPTER 2

MOROCCO AND ALGERIA

(Encounters with exotic and strange cultures) *6*

CHAPTER 3

The Sahara Desert

(Overwhelming heat and desolation)...*22*

CHAPTER 4:

Nigeria – The Cameroons – Central African Republic

(A welcome change of scenery)...*43*

CHAPTER 5

Zaire and the Congo (Into deepest, darkest Africa).........................*65*

CHAPTER 6

East Africa (Finally on Safari). *104*

CHAPTER 7

Nairobi - Mombasa - Lamu Island

(The Big City at last, and discovery of an Island Paradise) 127

CHAPTER 8

Mt. Kilimanjaro (Journey to the roof of Africa) 175

CHAPTER 9

Northern Kenya (Off the beaten path) 204

CHAPTER 10

Leaving Africa – Arriving London

(Goodbye to one world – hello to another) 241

CHAPTER 11

Returning Home

(Forever changed, and with memories for a lifetime 249

EPILOGUE

(From then to now – Changes in Africa since 1974-1975) 256

APPENDIX / ADDENDUM 258

PREFACE

Travels with King Kong–
How it all began and who was John?

In 1971, I was working as a forester on the Republic Ranger District in the Colville National Forest of northeast Washington state, after having completed 2 years of service with the US Army in Germany. That summer, a young high school teacher from Tacoma, named John, took the job of fire guard on Bodie Mountain lookout tower. Soon we became friends, but little did I know at the time, 3 years later the two of us would embark on a journey around the world. Two years passed, and while I was completing my master's degree in Environmental Planning at the University of Washington, John began planning our around the world trip. Since I was consumed in my studies and writing my thesis, John took on the task of making travel arrangements, starting with arranging for us to join an overland expedition traveling across Africa from Morocco to Nairobi. But before we could leave Seattle, there were visas to be obtained, several inoculations needed, and camping gear to be purchased—not to mention the submission of my thesis to the graduate school.

In late summer of 1974, I rushed feverishly to complete the final draft of my thesis, pack the essentials I thought I would need for traveling across the Sahara Desert and through the jungles of the Congo, as well as book a flight to Europe where I would meet up with John. It all happened in such a mad rush, it wasn't until John and I stepped off the ferry in

Tangiers that I finally realized I was headed into the unknown for who knew how long! A few days later, we met up with the SIAFU overland group camped on a beach south of Tangiers. This is where I met King Kong—he was an old British Army bus and little did I know then that he would hold a lifetime of memories for me!

What follows is my daily journal describing the journey—the places I saw, the people I encountered, the trials and tribulations I experienced, and the unforgettable moments that forever remain with me. Enjoy the trip!

INTRODUCTION

SIAFU Overland Expedition - What was it like?

[Meeting up with the group]

When John was investigating the options for overland travel, he found a couple of companies offering trips from London to Nairobi, one of them being SIAFU. He chose the company primarily because it was significantly less expensive than the other, something that would haunt us later. When we arrived in Morocco, we met up with the SIAFU group who were camped on a beach south of Tangiers. The majority of overland travelers in the group were young and single—only two married couples. The group was pretty much equally divided between men and women. Among the countries they represented were the UK/ Scotland, Australia, New Zealand, Canada, and the USA. There were close to 35 people signed on for the trip, including a few notable characters that later I would come to remember for a long time. Among them was an elderly couple named Mr. and Mrs. Barton Smith from New Zealand. Mr. Smith had a wooden leg and would become known as "Bartie". Then there were the "New Yorkers" who would become famous for their continual "bitching" about almost everything during the trip. They were joined by a middle-aged Jewish man named Simon, also from New York City. He would become a very "high maintenance" traveler. As fortune would have it, there were four Johns in the group, Scottish John, English John, Canadian John, and of course American John! And then there was a very pretty English girl who immediately caught my attention and who would later become a significant part of my experience on the journey across Africa.

[Responsibilities in the group]

There were two old British military vehicles, an old Bedford truck and a rundown Bedford bus nicknamed "King Kong". They were driven by two experienced overland drivers, Stuart and Joe. The group had been divided into "crews" for the trip, and when John and I showed up, we were assigned jobs for the journey, as had everyone else. Since we were the last to join the group, the only jobs remaining were with the cooking crews, whose responsibility was to cook dinner every evening. They also did the shopping in local markets along the way to supplement dehydrated meals with fresh produce and fruit, where available. The other jobs on the expedition were (a) loading and unloading of gear and supplies each morning and evening, (b) gathering of firewood and making the campfire each evening (gathering of camel dung in the desert), and (c) checking fluid levels, tires, and overall vehicle maintenance, otherwise known as "mechanic". After a couple of days, I traded jobs with Krem, a young guy from a wealthy family in the jewelry business, and I became the mechanic for the rest of the journey.

[Camping and Travelling]

Virtually every evening during our 5-month journey, we camped out in tents, whether at a campground in a town, in the middle of the desert, or deep in the jungle, where many times we camped on the edge of a small village. The only exceptions were a few rare occasions when John would find a cheap hotel for the night. After a few days on the road the group divided itself into those who rode in the back of the truck and those of us who rode inside the bus. The truck was outside seating and often very dusty and windy, whereas seating inside the bus could be very hot and stuffy at times. Being that I was the mechanic on the trip, Stuart invited me to sit upfront in the bus with him, which afforded me a great view of the road ahead. It was a view that the people riding in the truck rarely had. The bus had a large side door and often we would stand in the open doorway to wave at people as we passed through villages. And people everywhere almost always waved back to us!

[Food and Water]

As far as food and water was concerned, we began the journey with a large stock of dry and dehydrated food that was supplemented with fresh produce and fruit from local village markets along the way, where avail- able. Each vehicle also carried a dozen 5-gallon jerry cans of water, which were filled at wells and local water supplies along the route. The water had to be disinfected with chlorination tablets, which turned the water "putrid" tasting in the extreme desert heat! Breakfast was always one of four different kinds of dry cereal, along with condensed milk, while lunch was usually canned meat and crackers. Dinner in the evening was cooked over an open campfire and consisted of one of five different dehydrated meals, such as "farmer's stew", "mac and cheese", or "chicken delight"! Needless to say, the lack of variety became frustrating after a month or so, especially crossing the Sahara Desert where there were no local markets to supplement our diet.

[Communications]

The only way to describe communications with the outside world is to say there was NO communication for much of the trip. Letters from home had to be sent to the SIAFU office in London and then forwarded to "Poste Restante" in a few major cities on the route to await our arrival. We travelled for well over 6 weeks before arriving in Kano, Nigeria where we picked up the first batch of letters from home. And regarding the posting of letters and post cards to family and friends back home as we travelled, it was always "unpredictable" whether or not they would arrive at their intended destination. (on a side note, upon returning home I found that my mother had saved every letter and post card I had sent!)

With the rare exception of being in a large town, there was NO access to radio, TV, newspapers, or magazines. So, the times we were able to find a newspaper or magazine, we read every page, cover to cover, especially an International Herald Tribune or Time Magazine! During the entire journey across the Sahara Desert, through the jungles of the Congo, and across the vast plains of East Africa, we had no way to contact anyone, except whenever we came to a large town, and that was generally by a very unreliable, and incredibly expensive international telephone call or Telex message. In 1974, there were NO cell phones, personal computers, mobile devices or the Internet!

[Entertainment]

And as far as recorded music was concerned, my little cassette tape player, with a half dozen tapes, was the only source during the entire 5-month trip. Despite the very limited musical library, I never tired of it. One tape in particular, "Dark Side of the Moon" by Pink Floyd, became a legend by the end of the journey. Almost every time we encountered a mechanical breakdown, which was quite often, Pink Floyd was there to keep us company as we made the repairs!

[Health and Hygiene]

It wasn't long before many of us began to experience the typical health issues inherent in traveling through third world countries. At one time or another, and sometimes more than one time, virtually everyone came down with a case of diarrhea. Usually it wasn't serious, but certainly not welcome and a frustrating experience. Of more concern was dysentery, which affected a few of us while we were stranded in the middle of the Sahara! Fortunately, there were no medical emergencies or serious diseases encountered during our 5-month journey.

Regarding hygiene, it must be said that "showers" were virtually nonexistent during our 6-week crossing of the Sahara Desert, as we had barely enough water each day to wash our hands and the dinner dishes each evening. Drinking water had to be rationed every day, which became a serious issue for some people during the intense heat of the desert. But once we had entered the jungle, we had many opportunities to bath in rivers and streams while we were camped. As for washing clothes, it was a real luxury when the opportunity presented itself. More often than not, we wore the same clothes for many days at a time, especially while we travelled across the desert. As a group, we became "accustomed" to our less than hygienic conditions, but I'm sure it must have been a rather "unpleasant" experience for others when we would arrive in a village or town—though no one really objected to our presence.

[Toilet Rites]

In the early stages of the journey, especially in the remote, barren wasteland of the Sahara Desert, when- ever we made a "pit stop", the women went to one side of the vehicles and the men to the other side. In the beginning, everyone walked a good distance away, often several hundred yards, in an attempt to seek some privacy! But as time went on, that distance became shorter and shorter, especially for the men! At the beginning of the trip, everyone had been given just two rolls of toilet paper. For most people that ran out in a few weeks and most of us resorted to collecting toilet paper from any restaurant or hotel in whatever town we came to.

The rule for relieving oneself whenever we were camped in the desert or the jungle, involved digging a hole with one of the camp shovels and covering it up with sand or soil afterwards. At some point during the trip, a small group of ladies began gathering together for their daily "toilet rites". They soon became known as the "Loo Group"! (Loo is the British slang for toilet, and a roll of toilet paper is known as a "bum roll", since the British slang for one's posterior is "bum") It was fascinating to watch the Loo Group gather on the edge of camp with bum rolls and shovel in hand, and make their journey into the countryside. However, no one outside the group ever witnessed their ritual!

Chapter One

September 6, 1974
Seattle, WA ("Happy Birthday" to me!)

"*Let the Journey Begin*" I woke up this morning finally feeling like I was going on a long-awaited trip— not just any ordinary trip mind you. This was a trip conceived some several months earlier as part of a grand daydream with my friend John. He talked of traveling around the world, starting in Africa. Here I was facing a trip of some undetermined length and not even a bag was packed for my departure today. With a few deliberate motions I rounded up some of the most obvious items of clothing I would need for the Sahara Desert and the tropical rainforests I was about to encounter in the next few months. As the clothes were stuffed into the huge forest green rucksack, I had purchased the week before, I thought back over the past three weeks spent laboring with my master's degree thesis. As the days had approached the present, I had nightmares of an unfinished piece of work during the few hours I had to catch any sleep. It was something that would later haunt me throughout my journey to far-off lands.

Even on the last night before my departure, I had barely enough time to finish the last minute instructions to my good friend Joan about how to make sure the typing was completed and proofed, the reproductions finished and placed in their correct position, the requisite number of copies made and delivered to the Graduate School, and several other tasks to accomplish which would enable me to graduate from the university. By the time all the formalities and regulations had been complied with and my degree awarded, I would be somewhere between Morocco and Nigeria! But had I thought of everything? And what if I hadn't, how would anyone get in touch with me? Suddenly all the anxiety of the past three months rushed through my body and I quivered for a moment. My eyes darted to the clock on my desk and the realization that my plane to Europe would be departing in less than three hours jolted me back to reality.

My Passport

There was a bag to finish packing, arrangements to be confirmed, and a final farewell to a few friends. A week prior, I had located a nice family in Edmonds to adopt Ming, my beloved Sealpoint Siamese. It had been a difficult, emotional moment when I handed him over to the family who would give him his new home. The emotions of that moment stayed with me for many weeks later as I travelled through foreign lands.

As I stuffed the last few precious essentials into my bulging green rucksack, a knock on the door startled me. Upon opening it, I found the bright and beautiful face of my friend Marta who had graciously volunteered to take me to the airport. It was a delight to see her and to know someone was going to send me off on my journey to the Dark Continent. We loaded my bag into Marta's Volkswagen and headed for the freeway. The long ride to the airport was broken by the excited questions Marta asked of my plans for the upcoming months in Africa. I did my very best to answer them as specifically as possible, but I had no better realization of what was in store for me than she. I left Seattle aboard an Eastern Airlines flight bound for Chicago where I would connect with a flight to Europe on Icelandic Airlines, the least expensive ticket available.

Since I had an overnight stay in Chicago, I called my friend Steve who lived downtown in a new high-rise apartment building overlooking Lake Michigan. Steve and I had spent a summer together working on the Beaverhead National Forest in southwest Montana, during which we spent many nights in the bars of West Yellowstone. When Steve met me at O'Hare airport, he had no idea of my plans to travel overland across Africa, so there were a lot of questions I had to try and answer that night as we sat on the balcony with our beer. The next morning Steve took me back to the airport and I boarded the Icelandic Airlines flight to Luxembourg, and as an added bonus, there was a short stopover in Reykjavík early the following morning.

"A Train to Madrid" Upon arrival in Luxembourg I headed for the train station to buy a ticket to Madrid where I was to meet up with John. He had been working in Spain for several weeks teaching English as a second language. When the railway station agent handed me a single small ticket stub that read "LUX—MAD" I assumed it meant a through train. But once on board the train a friendly American girl living in Paris struck up a conversation, and upon hearing that I was on my way to Madrid she told me I would have to change stations in Paris, which came as a complete surprise to me. Seeing the anxious look on my face, she graciously offered me a Paris Metro ticket, along with instructions about how to get from Gare du Nord to Gare du Est. (Her act of kindness proved to be a lifesaver!) I successfully negotiated the Paris Metro system at the height of the evening rush hour and arrived at Gare du Est. Then it was a matter of trying to find the right train going to Madrid.

After several unsuccessful attempts to ask the station staff for help, I suddenly saw a sign that had "Madrid" written on it, along with the names of several other places. I had to run down the platform with my overloaded backpack to board the train moments before it departed the station that night. Finally, on board I found the train so crowded that I had to sit on my backpack in the aisleway, along with a lot of other passengers. After an hour or so the conductor came through the carriage checking tickets and when he saw mine, he rattled off something in French. Seeing my confused look, a kind old man nearby translated it to inform me that I was in the wrong car, since the train would split in Toulouse in the middle of the night. So, I was instructed to walk to the other end of the train. After struggling to lug my heavy backpack through crowded aisles for several cars I finally found one empty seat in a crowded compartment and tried my best to get some sleep sitting up.

Daylight came all too early and soon the train approached the Spanish border at a small, non-descript building. I followed the other passengers as they all got off the train and proceeded through a door marked "Customs and Immigration". Then, rather than going back out the same door to re-board our train, we had to exit through another door that now put us in Spain, on the opposite side of the station. (Since the gauge of the railroad tracks in Spain are wider than in the rest of Europe, we had to change to another train.) As I looked at the big board listing the schedule of departing trains, my heart sank—the next regular train to Madrid didn't leave until the next day! There was only one train leaving today and it was the all First Class "Talgo Express", and obviously my little ticket stub wasn't meant for First Class travel. After pleading with the ticket agent to accept all my remaining French Francs, he somehow took pity on me and gave me the ticket upgrade for travel on the Talgo.

As I boarded the luxury train and settled in my seat, I could feel the piercing eyes, like sharp daggers, from the other passengers around me, who were much more elegantly dressed. But for the next four hours I enjoyed the luxurious service and savored the gourmet food and wine that came with the First-Class travel experience. I arrived in Madrid well after 11:00pm and immediately went in search of a pay phone to call John who was staying with a family for the summer. After several calls with no answer, a policeman pointed me to another pay phone at a bar nearby, since the station was closing for the night. Finally, just before 1:00am John answered and was very surprised to learn that I had arrived at the Talgo station since he figured I wouldn't be travelling First Class. Apparently, he had checked the other train stations earlier in the evening and then assumed I wouldn't be arriving until the next day. So, he and his host family had decided to spend the evening at an amusement park.

CHAPTER TWO

September 12, 1974 Tangiers, Morocco

"*Stories from the Kasbah*" John and I ended up staying in a small hotel room for 6 dirham a night (about $1.50) which was incredibly cheap. But everything in Tangiers was cheap, at least for us anyway. We were staying in the "Kasbah", the old part of the city where things were still very much as they had always been in the past

"Kasbah" in Tangiers, Morocco

The little kids hustled us at every turn or glance. They sold everything from toy camels to dope. They instantly knew your nationality and would begin speaking your language, which was remarkable. They were very persistent but also polite and joking around. The trick was to play their game and be firm but polite in turning them away. Bargaining in the street market was the same way, only more so. Tangiers was a wonderfully exciting place, but also mysterious and a bit scary at times. I came to be fascinated by it. We ate in real authentic Arabic "greasy spoon joints" where the food was delicious. And over the next few days, I began looking forward more and more to the rest of the trip.

One day, while we were walking around the Kasbah, John saw some traditional Moroccan "slippers" and began bargaining for a pair. They were mostly gaudy bright colors and not very comfortable or easy for walking in the streets of Tangiers. But John was always one to enjoy fitting in with the local culture. One of the delights of our time in Tangiers was a glass of fresh brewed traditional mint tea, which was drunk hot, while holding a cube of sugar between the front teeth, so the tea was slowly sweetened as it was sipped— delicious! Our hotel room was very small and basic, with my first introduction to the "Gaelic" toilet—a hole in the floor with two small pedestals that functioned as "footrests" while using the toilet. They were also employed when taking a shower in the toilet! It was a very efficient use of space, but not very comfortable or particularly hygienic. But at the end of the day, we made the best of the undesirable situation.

After a few days, we made our way down to Asilah Beach south of the city where we met up with the SIAFU overland group. They had been camped on the beach for a couple of days before heading for Fez and Marrakech.

Asilah Beach, Morocco

The campground was highly developed, including several shops, toilets, a bar and even a nightclub! But the whole place was quite barren and looked more like a K-Mart parking lot than a campground. Lots of local vendors were plying their trade on the beach, peddling everything from the essentials, like bottled water and sun lotion, to the "unnecessary"—toy camels and cheap trinkets! We were introduced to the group and assigned our responsibilities during the trip, as had everyone else already. It wasn't long before John met some local guys on the beach, and we were invited to join them for dinner in the nightclub. I found them to be very curious about the world beyond Morocco, especially America. (John was always anxious to meet the locals and absorb as much of the culture as possible) Asilah Beach was also my first experience with diarrhea, and unfortunately not my last.

September 18, 1974
Asilah Beach to Fez, Morocco

"Moroccan Campgrounds and French Toilets" As we left Asilah Beach, John and I were officially part of the SIAFU Overland group and headed to the fabled city of Fez. The five days we had spent camped on the

beach in Asilah had been very pleasant and a comfortable introduction to Morocco. But now we were about to discover the heart of the country in Fez and Marrakesh and everyone was excited at the prospect. Seating in the truck was already fully occupied, so John and I joined the group riding in the bus. That turned out to be in our favor, since riding in the back of the truck was often dusty and exposed to the elements. As we made our way inland from the coast toward Fez, the countryside was mostly hot, dry, and barren in places, until we reached the foothills of the High Atlas Mountains and the city of Fez.

Late in the afternoon, we pulled into a large "campground" near the center of the old city. It was "typical" of most Moroccan campsites, often looking like a giant K-Mart parking lot, but with lots of bare ground, rocks, and a few small bushes instead of asphalt. It came complete with a small café, food store, and even a bar! ("Camp Africa" in Asilah Beach even had some native huts and a "discotheque"!) Although it was called "camping", the site appeared a lot more like a trailer park and tent city for refugees. Clothes lines were strung up everywhere, music blared constantly, old vehicles seemed to have been abandoned, and the smell of garbage was overwhelming at times! Besides the availability of toilets and washing facilities, the only saving grace was the convenient location near the old town market. Following my first visit to the toilets, which were the French ("Gaelic") design, all I could say was, "what a god-awful, ridiculous contraption on which to take a shit!" For those who never had the chance to use one, the instructions were to "squat" over the porcelain basin, "align" feet with the two foot pads, and "aim" for a small hole in the center! Needless to say, it was awkward, very uncomfortable, and definitely not conducive to a long period of contemplation! And to compound the situation, the toilets were very often a disgusting mess, lacking toilet paper, and nothing but a hassle. In my opinion, they were not the highest state of the art in bathroom fixtures. Graffiti in the toilets read, "French toilets are for yoga freaks"!

In spite of the horrible condition of the campsite in Fez, we found the old city to be a beautiful, ancient, wonderful experience as we wandered among hundreds of small shops in the huge open-air market, where one could find literally anything for sale.

Old walled city of Fez, Morocco

The section of the market devoted to the tanning of hides and processing of leather was amazing. Row upon row of circular vats filled with noxious chemicals and colored dyes spanned a large area where hides were rendered and tanned to make raw leather for manufacture into finished leather goods for which Fez was world famous. But the laborers who toiled in the vats must have suffered some horrible effects of the chemicals they had to endure as they worked the hides with their bare hands and feet.

While I enjoyed the experience of discovering the beautiful sights and delights of Fez, the diarrhea I suffered later was not enjoyable! It became my first lesson about the necessity of being cautious with local foods, and especially local sources of water. It was a very uncomfortable lesson, but one well learned!

September 19, 1974
Fez, Morocco to Marrakech, Morocco

"Lost in the Grand Bazaar" We left the Fez campsite early in the morning, bound for "another" Moroccan campsite in the mysterious city of Marrakesh. We had high expectations for our visit to the magical city, but it was not to be so. The drive among the foothills in the shadow of the High Atlas Mountains was very scenic. We passed through many small villages and towns that had remained much the same for centuries. After a pleasant trip from Fez to Marrakesh, we faced a couple of days camped in a less than desirable Moroccan campground, and its typical "amenities" of a café, store, bar, and French toilets! John and I had really been looking forward to exploring the old city, especially the Grand Bazaar, the largest open-air market in North Africa. But as we made our way through the old city gate, we quickly realized it was a giant maze of narrow streets and alleyways, and we had no map! Even a compass would have been useless within the chaotic layout of pathways that often came to a dead end. And all the while, as we "wandered" among rows and rows of small shops and stalls, the sights and sounds were fascinating. But, the continual pressure from the shop keepers to buy things became too much to bear, especially so when many of them grabbed our arm, trying to pull us into their shop.

After a while, I began to feel paranoid that every man, woman, and child was out to get me to buy something, even if it was something I didn't want or even needed! It seemed there was no possible way to convince them I didn't want to buy anything! Later, I felt there must have been some very nice people in the market, but we never encountered them. Finally, after enduring more than three hours of the hassle, we decided to leave the market as soon as possible. But the question was how to do so, since by that time we had no idea where we were or where the exit gate was located! So, what were we to do—no map and no idea of which way to turn? I believe we could have spent the rest of the day and night searching for a way out and been unsuccessful. Just then, a young boy approached us and asked if we needed help. Right away, John and I said "yes—how do we get to the main gate of the old city?" We negotiated (bargained) a very reasonable price and were led out of the market. Later, back at the campground, we both realized we had experienced a unique view of Marrakesh, but at the same time, we were looking forward to seeing another, more enjoyable side of Morocco.

September 22, 1974
Marrakech to Todra (Todgha) Gorge

"Over the High Atlas Mountains" After two days of non-stop hassle and another case of diarrhea, we left Marrakech, headed northeast over the High Atlas Mountains. Our destination was the eastern province of Morocco and the beginning of the Sahara Desert.

Berbers going to market

The feeling among the majority of our group was one of relief at leaving behind crowded cities and excitement about the challenge of crossing the Sahara. It was a long slow climb up to the summit of the High Atlas Mountains on a very steep, twisting road.

High Atlas Mountains, Morocco

Crossing the High Atlas Mountains

The route took us through lush pine forests and past small towns and villages, many with very old buildings that resembled ancient fortresses, with old stone parapets. The medieval character of their design made it difficult to tell the age of the buildings or the towns. I felt it was certainly one of the most scenic parts of Morocco. As we reached the summit at 5,200 feet elevation, we stopped to take in the spectacular views.

At the same time, we looked down at the road descending below us, and we knew we would be in for a "hair-raising" ride down to the desert!

After a couple of hours of "white-knuckle" driving, we reached the foot of the mountains and the very dry, barren, rocky landscape of eastern Morocco.

Descending the road to eastern Morocco

Then, all of a sudden, seemingly out of nowhere, a brief, but intense rainstorm descended upon us— the first sight of any rain in over two weeks of traveling in Morocco. A short time later, we came to a massive red rock gorge and a large oasis at the end of a very narrow canyon of high rock walls, in some places towering over 1,200 feet above us. Tall palm trees and lush green grass greeted us as we arrived at the Todra (Todgha) Gorge Hotel.

Hotel in Todra Gorge

That evening we were invited to "camp" on top of the hotel roof. It wasn't long before some of the local people arrived from the village to provide music and dance for the evening. The sounds of their woodwinds and drums were beautiful, especially as the cool night air surrounded us. A good time was had by all, particularly the villagers who danced with us. Soon the ugly memories of Marrakech began to fade away, and we looked forward to our meeting with the Sahara Desert in the morning.

September 24, 1974
Todra (Todgha) Gorge to Figuig, Morocco

"On the Edge of the Sahara" We left the Todra (Todgha) Gorge in the morning and travelled northeast to the small town of Figuig, on the border with Algeria. We had a few minor mechanical problems with the vehicles, especially the old bus, nicknamed "King Kong", but otherwise the trip went well. The plan was to cross the border into Algeria and find a suitable campsite along the road. But as we were preparing for the border crossing, one of our drivers discovered he had lost his passport! After a few minutes, he realized he had accidently left it at the campground in Asilah Beach several days earlier. So, Dave and Stuart went to the police station in Figuig and asked to have the police in Asilah Beach recover Dave's passport. Luckily, after a few hours, the police reported the passport had been found and would be delivered to Figuig in a couple of days.

In the meantime, John had scouted out the small town and found a cheap hotel for the equivalent of 65 cents a night! The room wasn't five star, but it did have a toilet and shower—the toilet and shower being one in the same! It also had a nice view overlooking the main street.

Overlooking Main street in Figuig, Morocco

17

The town was located in a large oasis, surrounded by tall date palms. As John and I explored the small town, it became clear we were here during "Ramadan", the most important religious celebration in Islam. Observance by the local Muslims was very traditional and strict. Virtually every woman on the street was tightly veiled, with some of them completely hidden beneath long robes, veils, and even black gloves, despite the hot weather. Although the town was very religious and quite conservative, it was also very friendly, with none of the hassle we had experienced elsewhere in Morocco.

Children on the street in Figuig, Morocco

The surrounding countryside was very dry and almost barren, yet we saw small herds of camels and goats grazing on the scrubby grass and bushes. During the heat of the day, everything and everyone seemed to move more slowly. Between noon and 4pm, when the heat of the sun was most intense, activity on the street almost came to a complete stop! The time we spent in Figuig was pleasant, though quite hot and very quiet. So, after a couple of days, we were all looking forward to moving on. In the late afternoon of the second day, Dave's passport arrived at the police station, but by that time the Algerian border station had closed for the night. We had dinner around the campfire that night and talked about our expectations of beginning the crossing of the Sahara Desert the next day. The crossing through Algeria and Niger to Nigeria was scheduled to take almost a week. But little did we know that evening, we would be in for a much longer journey through the desert!

September 26, 1974
Figuig, Morocco to Algeria

"Welcome to Algeria and the Sahara Desert" The next morning, we drove to the other end of town and approached the Algerian Border Post. The border crossing involved lots of paperwork and red tape, but having 37 people in our group, we expected it. The slow pace of work in the desert heat didn't do anything to speed up the process either. The border crossing was made more complicated because the Immigration officials couldn't read many of our foreign passports. Luckily, several people in our group spoke some French and "assisted" the officials. After several hours, we were finally allowed into Algeria! Our route southeast followed a paved highway through the desert, and we spotted our first sight of large sand dunes— the classic image of the Sahara. Along the way, the local people were quite friendly, yet very curious at the same time. We encountered none of the hassle we had experienced in Morocco. My impression was that few tourists ever made it to the remote parts of Algeria. All of us felt it was a very welcome change indeed.

That evening, we pulled off the highway and found a nice level spot at the foot of some rocky hills to set up camp on the sand.

Camped in the Sahara Desert, Algeria

All around us were small, round things that looked like rocks. But in fact, they were little mounds of sand covered in a tiny form of vegetation—very strange things for sure. They virtually crumbled into dust at the slightest touch! Being in the middle of such a barren landscape, with virtually no vegetation in sight, our campfire crew had to resort to collecting small clumps of dried camel dung as a source of fire. And it turned out to be a very effective source of heat for cooking. For the next several weeks, camel dung would be our primary campfire resource!

September 27, 1974

(somewhere north of Bechar, Algeria)

"The Experience of a Desert Oasis" Early the next morning, we were back on the road, headed south toward Bechar, Algeria—a small town at the end of the paved road. The day was very hot and the thirst for water was intense, although the supply we carried in the large 5-gallon jerry cans quickly became hot and tepid. Along with the disagreeable taste of the water purification tablets, it didn't do much to "quench our thirst"! Late in the afternoon, a couple of Algerian motorcycle policemen came by and said they would show us a beautiful oasis just a few miles ahead, where we could camp for the night. We arrived to find a lovely area of tall palm trees and plenty of water in the well.

While the campfire and cooking crew prepared dinner, a few of us hiked up to a nearby hilltop where we discovered a series of old stone guard towers built by the French army decades ago.

Abandoned French fort, Algeria

We could see for many miles in the light of the full moon. There was also an old abandoned French fort at the base of the hill. As I sat in one of the abandoned guard towers, listening to beautiful music from my cassette tape player, and gazing upon the moonlit landscape below, I could almost imagine it was a scene from "Lawrence of Arabia"! At that moment, I almost expected to see a legion of Arabs on horseback in the distance! After dinner, several of us stripped down under the moonlight, and took turns throwing buckets of water over each other! It was a magical experience to let the warm night air dry our bodies. After a hot, dry, dusty day, it was a most refreshing and natural experience. As I stood naked and wet under the moonlight in the warm desert night, I felt a "oneness" with the world! After the "rejuvenation" of the "water worship", sleep came quickly and softly as I lay in my sleeping bag on the sand. A beautiful moment in my memory of the Sahara Desert!

Chapter Three

September 28, 1974
(somewhere in the middle of the Sahara Desert)

"*Remote and Alone*" After a full day of driving across barren and remote desert, the night fell upon us rather suddenly. We barely had enough time to pull over and set up camp in the middle of the Sahara.

The site was as flat as anyone could imagine, and devoid of any vegetation, or any sign of life, for that matter. As we prepared for supper, a short, but intense windstorm descended upon us. After supper, Rob and I walked up the dirt road for a couple of miles, in the direction of a small speck of light and discovered a tiny café where we enjoyed a cup of hot tea. Strangely, there was not another building in sight for miles in any direction! Soon, Rob was smoking hash with the owner, and later, a couple of Algerian policemen stopped by. They knew the owner well, and claimed Algerian policemen only did humanitarian work, just arresting people who were endangering others—which was very fortunate for Rob, as he continued to smoke hash! As the evening came to a close, Rob and I were offered a ride back to our camp with some Algerian Army soldiers. We climbed into the cab of a huge French Berliat army truck. I counted seven of us in the cab, in addition to the driver! Looking back on that night, Rob and I were very lucky—we could never have planned such an adventure! The experience of that night in the middle of the Sahara remained an indelible memory of the desert!

September 30, 1974
(north of Ain Salah, Algeria)

"Flies in the Morning" Yesterday we camped out at a small water hole in the middle of another very barren region that became a wonderland at night—billions of stars filled the entire sky. That night, I took my sleeping bag and walked a few hundred yards away from camp into the desert. As I lay on the sand, staring up at the stars, I listened to some beautiful music from my cassette tape player. Time seemed to stop, and I felt as if I was the only one in the world at that moment. That experience of becoming one with the universe remained etched in my memory of the Sahara!

At 5:30am the next morning, we were rudely awakened by the sound of thunder and flash of lightning. Then it suddenly rained like hell for a few minutes and remained cloudy for the rest of the day. We spent the day traveling across very flat, barren, rocky desert terrain without seeing a single living thing, or anyone else for that matter.

Road to Ain Salah, Algeria

At times, we encountered images of distant mirages and dust devils on the horizon, which intensified the experience of being in the middle of the Sahara—a hundred miles from any sign of civilization! By the end of the day, I was beginning to feel the change I had been told to expect from confronting the desert on its own terms. I also began to better appreciate many things I had taken for granted before embarking on the overland trip—one of the most obvious was the precious nature of water and its scarcity! I was beginning to see the trip through new eyes.

Note: After several days of travelling in the desert of Algeria, I came to the conclusion that the oases had the most flies I had ever seen, anywhere! And it seemed as though, every fly had but one objective in mind—to perpetually force my attention to focus on its obvious buzz! And worst of all, they delighted in teasing and taunting me with the buzz and wind from their wings as they dived in and out of the range of my hand. They rarely had a bite, but they refused to leave, except under the most ardent circumstances. They were everywhere in the oases, throughout the day and night. But the time they enjoyed the most was pestering the shit out of me when I first awakened in the morning—it was an unbelievably rude and traumatic experience to be brought to consciousness by a fly "poking" his nose up my nose! Flies in the oases soon became a threat to my sanity!

Oasis in the Sahara Desert

October 2, 1974
Ain Salah, Algeria

"A Welcome Break" Late the next day, we arrived in the small, but strategic town of Ain Salah, about halfway to Kano, Nigeria and 150 miles from the next nearest town. It wasn't long before John found the one and only hotel in town, and soon afterwards, five of us rented a room for 5 dinars each (about $1.20). It came complete with 3 beds, an air conditioner that worked some of the time, a small shower, and at least a couple of cockroaches! We spent most of the evening relaxing in the air-conditioned room, listening to music on my cassette tape player, and sharing our experiences of being in the Sahara.

Ain Salah, Algeria

October 3-7, 1974
Ain Salah to Tamanrasset, Algeria

"A Hundred Miles from Nowhere" The route from Ain Salah to Tamanrasset was supposed to take two days, but due to several minor mechanical problems with the old bus, the journey took us four days. We followed the track of a UN Relief Agency truck convoy that had delivered food and medical supplies to several refugee camps the month before. During the daytime, we endured the intense heat and bone-dry weather, as best we could. As we drove across the very dusty, barren desert landscape, the experience made a strong impression upon me, especially the overwhelming thirst for a cold glass of water, or any cold drink for that matter! There were some moments when the mirage of a tall, cold double gin and tonic appeared before me, especially around midday when the heat of the desert reached burning proportions, and my canteen water had become hot and putrid from the chlorination tablets! But when night fell and the air suddenly cooled, the memories of the intense heat and barren land began to fade.

Finally, on the fourth day, we arrived in Tamanrasset, a remote government outpost in the middle of Algeria. Here we had planned to clean up, buy a few supplies, and be on our way to the Niger border. The immigration and customs formalities were brief, but as we were leaving the border post, one of our vehicles accidentally struck a guy wire supporting the Algerian Police radio antenna and bent it. So, we were instructed to set up camp at a small reservoir nearby and wait until the police could wire their headquarters in Algiers for instructions about how to handle the situation. We found the reservoir to be a lovely place to camp, having plenty of water for washing up and shade for relaxing. Even though we were now many days behind schedule, we all felt it was a great place for a break from the road. As I explored the area around the reservoir, I discovered a large number of birds in a marshy grove of palm trees—quite a dramatic contrast to the dry, dusty desert and barren mountains surrounding it. I took the opportunity to photograph Great

Blue Heron, Crested White Egret, and a couple of eagles. The marsh was like a tiny island of "life" in the middle of a "lifeless" world!

Later in the afternoon, clouds began to fill the sky and soon we felt the invigorating effect of a few light rain showers—the cooling of the desert air was remarkable and a very welcome relief from the hot sun and burning sand. As the raindrops softly touched my skin, I began to feel "homesick" for the rainy days in Seattle. That evening around the campfire, my thoughts were about how tough and grueling the trip it had been so far, and the many unknown challenges that surely lay ahead. Little did I know at that moment, just how tough and challenging it would become over the next several weeks. Yet, at the same time, I somehow knew it would also be a greater and more rewarding experience than I ever could have imagined. In the morning, we would continue our journey toward the ancient city of Agadez in the remote country of Niger. The next day, we were allowed to leave Tamanrasset, after paying a small fine. Stuart and Joe were very happy with the settlement, having feared a much harsher judgement from police headquarters in Algiers. Then it was another long day of driving across the desert, doing our best to cope with the intense heat and unending thirst for water. In the evening, we were fortunate to be able to set up camp on the edge of a tiny village called Amsel. Once again, the cool night air "washed" away our memories of the hot, dry, dusty day.

I came to look forward to the desert nights very much!

October 8-10, 1974
(somewhere between Tamanrasset and In-Guezzem)

"The Big Breakdown" Early in the morning, as the sun began its daily journey across the desert, we broke camp outside the small village of Amsel, and loaded up the old bus. There were backpacks and tents to be hoisted up the ladder to the roof rack, while cooking utensils and food supplies were packed back into the storage boxes inside the rear of the bus. And lastly, the 5-gallon water cans were placed back in the racks on the side of the bus. This procedure of breaking camp was virtually the same every day and had become a very familiar and well-choreographed routine. Then it was back on the road to drive as far as possible, following the rough track across the desert in the direction of Niger, a lonely country in the middle of the Sahara. We were having a pretty good day, having driven about 100 miles with only one minor mechanical problem with the steering assembly.

As the blazing sun slowly released its grip on the land, we found a level spot not far off the road, upon which to pitch our tents and setup camp for the night. Soon the heat of the day gave way to the cool of the evening, and we sat down to the usual dinner of rehydrated rations, of which there were only 5 different choices. But it was a time to chat amongst ourselves, recall the experiences of the day, and for me to write in my journal before darkness fell upon us. Sometimes I would walk out in the desert, away from camp, roll out my sleeping bag on the sand, and lay there just staring up at the billions of stars spread across the heavens—complete darkness and total silence!

At daybreak the next day, we once again broke camp, loaded the bus, and continued our slow, steady journey across the Sahara toward Niger. We had driven about 60 miles, when all of a sudden, the old bus lurched to one side and we knew we had encountered another mechanical problem for the umpteenth time! What could it be this time, I thought? As Stuart and I climbed under the vehicle, we could see one of the

28

heavy steel spring assemblies had broken. Luckily, we had a spare set for replacement, which took us 3 hours to replace.

Me replacing front spring assembly on King Kong in Sahara Desert

Feeling confident about the road ahead, we were off and running. Then just 10 miles further, the old girl suddenly came to a grinding halt, the engine sputtered for a moment and died! Stuart and I looked at each other with puzzled faces. Upon investigation, we found that one of the exhaust valves had dropped through the top of the piston—something we had no way to repair. Stuart suggested that we try to seal off the bad cylinder, which meant tearing down the top of the engine to access it. So, we set to work, and after a couple of hours we had completed the makeshift repair, much like a "bush mechanic" would do.

But after running a few miles, it was clear to both of us that the old girl would not pull the load over the rough road and soft sand. So, a decision was made to transfer as many people and as much gear as possible to the truck, which would then continue on to the next village, wherever that might be, for water and setup camp. Meanwhile, the rest of us prepared to setup camp where we were and await the return of the truck the next day. That evening, as we sat under the stars, we all had the feeling of being "stranded" in the middle of the Sahara. The feeling was made even more so by the fact that we had only a limited supply of water and there was no traffic on the road. It could have potentially become a dangerous, life-threatening situation if the truck were to break down as well!

Later, as night fell, the desert revealed its other side—a gorgeous sky filled with bright stars, a cool breeze, and the silhouettes of some weird rock formations. That night, everyone became a bit closer, sharing their hopes and fears—the trek across the Sahara had been a tremendously challenging experience, both physically and mentally. It had become a time where we learned a lot about ourselves and our traveling companions. The breakdown was not only a mechanical one, but also a personal one for many in the group. It was almost a climax point of frustration for some, especially with all of the mechanical problems, illness, and heat stress we had already endured. I also felt the stress of the journey, but perhaps less so than some of the group who had expected something more like a guided tour where everything was planned well in advance and with few surprises. Our trip had become the opposite of that and would become even more so as we continued through Africa.

Unknown grave in the Sahara

October 14-19, 1974
In-Guezzem, Algeria to Arlit, Niger

"On a Mission to Find Help" After a fitful night, I awoke with the sunrise, packed a small bag of travel essentials, and joined Joe and my two colleagues for the trip to Arlit. As the truck pulled out of the camp, I felt a sense of sorrow for those who had to remain behind. (It should be noted that John had previously hitched a ride with a UN truck before we left Tamanrasset, so who knows where we'll meet up again?) Late in the afternoon, we arrived in Arlit after a day of rough driving through roadless desert, following the tracks of a 100 truck UN convoy that had hauled food to remote villages the month before. The town of Arlit really surprised us with its size and sophistication. However, as we discovered, it was the center of a large French uranium mining operation and had many of the comforts and conveniences of home for the French staff and families living there. It wasn't long before we found cold beer, a bank, supermarket, and even a large swimming pool. Although we were welcome to shop in the French part of town, we were expected to camp in the old part, among the local people.

As we searched for a place to park the truck overnight, who should suddenly show up—John! He had already been in town for a few days and made friends with a local town elder, which turned out to be a blessing and marvelous stroke of luck for us. The elder invited us to park behind his house, and even insisted that we use his shower, toilet, and refrigerator while he would be out of town!

"Camped" in Arlit, Niger

What an amazing good fortune for us, and all due to John's incredible skills of meeting people! (To be able to sit down on an honest to goodness proper toilet was heavenly, especially after having spent weeks "squatting" on the desert sand!) The generosity of our local host was most welcome, and over the next several days, we found the local people to be very friendly and outgoing. Meanwhile, John got the "urge" to move on and landed a ride with a Nigerian truck headed south to Kano. Perhaps that's where we'll meet up again? Despite the relative luxury of being in Arlit, I came down with dysentery for the second time in over a month.

One night in particular, I felt as if I was going to die from the sickness. I spent the next couple of days suffering from severe diarrhea that completely sapped all my energy. It was even a struggle just to lie in bed, as I was so weak. I lost a significant amount of weight, which I could hardly afford to part with. At the same time, the heat of the mid-day sun seemed to drain the life from one's body and nullify the brain to the point where only a small measure of existence could be contemplated. I was even having some negative thoughts about continuing the trip. The constant mechanical problems, the desert heat, and now the recurring illness was weighing on me, as well as the group being so large. So, as time passed slowly in Arlit, I gave some thought to splitting from the group when we reached Kano, Nigeria and flying on to Nairobi. But I wondered if maybe my thoughts would change in time?

October 20 - 25, 1974
Arlit, Niger

"The Long Wait" Yesterday, Joe went to the office of the French mining company and was able to send a telex to the SIAFU office in London requesting parts to repair the engine in the bus. Their reply stated the parts would be shipped by air freight to the airport in Niamey, capitol of Niger. Luckily, Joe was able to secure a seat on the mining company's regular flight to Niamey the next day. Meanwhile, Krem, Robert, and I stayed behind with the truck, still parked behind the elder's house. We had made it our new home in Arlit. Every day was the same as the one yesterday and the one tomorrow and the next day—ad infinitum! We always arose at sunrise for breakfast to avoid the flies and the heat. Our meal was always cold cereal, condensed milk, bread, jam and hot tea. After breakfast, we cleaned up as best we could, straightened up things around the truck, and perhaps washed a few clothes. After which, I usually turned to reading a book, writing in my journal, or doing some letters and postcards to family and friends. The subject of the letters being how dull and boring it was doing the same thing day after day. By then it was time for lunch, which always consisted of tinned sardines, processed cheese, and perhaps bread. Then it was time for a nap during the hours when the sun's heat was most intense. As the day wore on into the late afternoon, there was more reading, writing and conversation, mostly about another dull, boring day that we had endured.

Later, as the sun made its way west toward the Atlantic Ocean, we were sometimes invited to take a shower in the house of our elder host, which was something to really appreciate after enduring the oppressive heat of the day. With the setting of the sun, we began preparations for dinner, which always consisted of some form of dehydrated food, all of which tasted basically the same. And if we were lucky, we had a couple of lukewarm beers from one of the numerous local food stands scattered along the main street. Following dinner, we did some cleanup of the truck and prepared to retire for the night. And to put the experience of the day into proper perspective, all our activities were conducted in view of a local audience—every kid who had nothing better to do than to sit for hours watching us fight boredom! It begged the question—if our day was boring, what was their day like when we weren't there? Then add 10 million flies and other assorted insects to the list of the day's participants! Despite the discomfort and boredom of being in Arlit, we were much more fortunate than those who had to spend their time in In-Guezzem! At last, Joe returned to Arlit with the Bedford truck parts to repair King Kong's engine, and we prepared for our return journey to In-Guezzem the next morning.

October 26 1974
Arlit, Niger Guezzem, Algeria

"Back to In-Guezzem"—*"Repairs in the Desert"* The following morning, we packed up our gear, and bade a fond farewell to the local elder whose warm generosity during the past week had been so welcome. Then we headed north out of town on the 220-mile return journey, following the rough track across the desert. At last, in the late afternoon, we arrived back at the SIAFU camp at In-Guezzem. I'm certain we were a very welcome sight for all those who had endured their time in camp. Stuart gave us a big hug, and then quickly turned his attention to completing an inventory of the spare parts we had delivered. Over dinner that evening, around the campfire, we shared our experiences of the past week in Arlit.

October 27-28 1974
In-Guezzem, Algeria

"A New King Kong" The next morning, Stuart, Joe and I began the task of repairing Kong's engine, something that required us to completely tear down the engine block to replace the piston, valves, and cylinder with

35

the new parts. It was very labor intensive and involved 12–14 hours of hard work for two days. And the incessant heat and wind that stirred up dust and sand all day long did nothing to help us. But eventually, we were successful, and the old girl finally leaped to life again! We were also able to repair the steering arm assembly in the process. At that point, we all hoped to be able to leave behind the bad memories of mechanical breakdowns and move on toward Nairobi with a renewed spirit and healthy King Kong!

That evening, as we sat around the campfire, I asked some of those who had remained at In-Guezzem about their experiences during the 12 days they were stuck in the camp. I was told the local Toureg people had been marvelous neighbors—having returned lost articles, traded their goods for old t-shirts, and provided some welcome cultural diversions in the form of traditional music, dance and even camel races! But it had also been a tough physical ordeal, having to put up with the intense desert heat, sandstorms, choking dust, lack of sanitary facilities, and above all, the overwhelming number of flies! I spent just 3 days in the camp and found it almost intolerable! So, to have suffered for nearly two weeks must have been unbearable!

October 29 1974
In-Guezzem, Algeria to Arlit, Niger

"On the Road Again" We arose with the sun, very early in the morning, and as one of the girls picked up a bag, a scorpion suddenly sprang up and she screamed. I immediately jumped up and stomped on it with my mountain climbing boots to save the day. At that point, I was finally beginning to feel physically fit again for the first time in many days and looking forward to getting back on the road again. As our group gathered all the gear for loading on the vehicles in preparation to depart the camp, I felt the local Toureg people were sad to see us leave. Our resident doctor and nurses had tended to many of them who were ill and must have won many friends. At the moment we left the village, I wondered what the local people would do once we were gone, for there was virtually nothing but a dirt road, a well for water, and the vast expanse of desert—200 miles from the nearest town or village!

From In-Guezzem, it was a five-hour drive back to Arlit where we would have a chance to pick up some fresh produce for the first time in several weeks. It would also be the opportunity to have some mechanical repairs completed at the French uranium mine machine shop. As we finally arrived in the town, we discovered a shop that had just received a shipment of fresh fruit.

Main street in Arlit, Niger

The tangerines and oranges appeared green on the outside, but they were surprisingly sweet inside. It was a real delight to taste something besides dehydrated food for a change. However, we found the entire town was out of Coke and beer—most disappointing, but not unusual in the middle of the Sahara! As we strolled along the main street, we came upon a silversmith's shop and watched the artist make the traditional "Agadez Cross"—a beautiful design very unique to Niger.

Agadez Cross

Several sales were made that day, and afterwards, a few us had lunch at a local restaurant called "Madame Zara's". Despite sounding like a shady whorehouse, Madame Zara fixed some really tasty food. She had only two items on the menu—rice with spicy sauce and rice with spicy meat sauce! Madame Zara was very welcoming to us, as were all the local people we encountered in Arlit.

Late in the day, Stuart and Joe returned from the machine shop, and we headed out of town to a nice campsite in the middle of the sand and rock, much as we had done everywhere else in the desert. But just after pitching our tents, the wind suddenly came up like a howling banshee, and within a few minutes,we were engulfed in a full-blown sandstorm! It only lasted a couple of hours, but it felt like we were in the middle of a red-hot furnace being blasted with tons of burning sand! As the wind finally died down, there was a thick layer sand covering everything— we were literally eating, breathing, and sleeping in the stuff. During the height of the sandstorm, all I could do was sit in the lee of the tent and resign myself to being "one with the desert". With the sandstorm over, we sat down to dinner around the campfire and enjoyed a calm, quiet, cool evening. Our next destination would be the fabled city of Agadez, on our continued journey south to Kano, Nigeria.

October 30, 1974
Arlit, Niger to Agadez, Niger

"Leaving the Desert Behind" The following morning, as the sun rose on the horizon,

Sunrise in the Sahara Desert

I popped my head out of the tent and an amazing image appeared before me. In the distance, on the edge of our camp, stood a Toureg man next to his camel. He seemed very curious, but also very shy, hiding behind his camel. Just after I reached for my camera and snapped a photograph, he disappeared into the dim light of the early morning. It was a picture of a single moment in time. An hour later, we broke camp, loaded the vehicles, and began our journey toward Agadez. As we left Arlit, I noticed a dramatic change in the landscape. North of Arlit had been a barren desert, as had been the case throughout Algeria. Yet, south of the town, I began seeing a scattering of small bushes and a few clumps of grass.

A few miles further south, as we crossed over some low hills, we came upon whole fields of grass and small groves of trees—which would become thicker and more numerous the further south we travelled. Joe said that on his most recent trip through the region a few months before, it had been as barren as the desert in the north. Apparently, significant rains had arrived within the past two months and given rise to the lush vegetation almost overnight. We had officially entered a part of Africa known as the "Sahel". But it would take more than a few inches of rain to conquer the disastrous effects of several years of drought in the region. A few United Nations refugee camps for the region's nomadic people, like the Toureg, still remained around larger towns and villages. The drought had also been responsible for higher prices and shortages of goods, even the most basic staple items. As I gazed upon the emerging landscape, I was hopeful it was a sign of a long-term recovery.

But as we approached Agadez, something seemed out of order. The road had been quite rough, however, Kong appeared to be bouncing around more than usual. Stuart stopped outside the town and we investigated the situation. As bad luck would have it, we found both main front spring assemblies had broken beyond repair! We had no replacements, so our only hope was to find them somewhere in Agadez. The prospect of locating two of the parts in the small town was nearly impossible! But unbelievably, Stuart found a local mechanic who claimed he could get two main front spring assemblies for us later that day. And sure enough, we were lucky he arrived with the parts as promised. We set about installing them as soon as possible in order to make an early departure the next morning.

Our time in Agadez was marked by a great deal of hassle from the locals to buy anything and everything, much in contrast to our experience in Arlit. While I saw some nice stuff in the markets, the pressure to buy was overwhelming, and it turned me off from purchasing anything! And at the same time, it was virtually impossible to find a place or time to be alone—it seemed like no matter where we went, there was an "audience" waiting to watch our every move. After a while, we began to feel we were "on display", as if we were in a zoo! Perhaps they had nothing else to do but stare at the tourists (us)? Later, upon reflection, I came to the realization, no matter how much I disliked being seen as a tourist, being a white man in black Africa it was inescapable. So, I resolved to bear with it and try to find some enjoyment in my role as a "tourist"!

Meanwhile, John had met an old Frenchman by the name of Joyce, and we were invited to camp at his oasis, "Joyce's Garden", a few miles outside of Agadez. It was a delightful place, with showers, toilets, swimming pool, and even a bar, that just happened to be out of everything at that moment. A lovely shady grove of trees sheltered our tents from the intense desert heat, and the number of flies was certainly tolerable, especially when compared to our experience with the oases in Algeria. That evening, as we shared dinner by the campfire, we exchanged stories of our time in Agadez. That was when Stuart confided in me that the mechanic had stolen the parts from a British Army truck!

October 31, 1974
Agadez, Niger – Kano, Nigeria

"Halloween" We awoke with the sunrise that morning, as usual, and I suddenly realized it was Halloween. Although, I was sure nobody in this part of the world knew anything about the holiday. As we left Joyce's Garden, our old bus was complete with new front spring assemblies, compliments of the British Army, though I was certain they were unaware of the loss, at least for the next few days. As we drove further south, the landscape continued to come to life before our eyes. It was

like the awakening of spring, and wonderful to see after so many weeks travelling through the barren expanse of the Sahara.

As we travelled to Zinder, about halfway to Kano, Nigeria, the land really began to come to life—trees became larger and more numerous, the grass greener and more abundant, and the signs of animal life became clearly evident. The memories of barren sand and rock in the Sahara Desert were rapidly retreating from our minds. The new, fresh, lush landscape spawned a feeling of uplifted spirit, as if we had been rejuvenated after a long thirst for life. The smell and feel of moisture in the air was very welcome, as was the noticeable decrease in the heat. That evening we camped just south of Zinder, and as we set up camp, not far off the road, the talk around the campfire was all about the desire to partake of the pleasures and luxuries that we anticipated in Kano, which had been denied to us for so long. There was a renewed energy and optimism among our group as we retired to our tents for the night, knowing that tomorrow we would be in Kano, Nigeria's second largest city.

CHAPTER FOUR

November 1, 1974
Kano, Nigeria

"A *Return to Civilization* " From our camp outside Zinder, it was only a few hours' drive before we arrived in Kano. As we slowly made our way toward the center of the city, we found it to be quite urbane and modern, in stark contrast to the remote expanse of the Sahara. Although we saw some signs of affluence, a vision of the underlying poverty of a majority of the people was evident everywhere. It was a big shock to come out of the desert experience of isolation, without contact with civilization, and then suddenly encounter the hustle and bustle of a large city. But, none the less, it was a welcome change. We made a stop at the Post Office our highest priority, and it was like a transfusion of home, to be able to read letters from family and friends. I had been looking forward to that moment ever since leaving Seattle two months before. It was so good to hear news from my parents and friends, especially the good news that my master's degree thesis had been accepted by the Graduate School— its fate had been up in the air as I had left Seattle. After savoring the letters and news from home, our thoughts turned to International news. We were able to get copies of the latest newspapers and magazines—the entire contents of which we read over the next few days. It was an attempt to satisfy our hunger for the recognition of life beyond the immediate boundaries of sight and sound.

After the Post Office stop, we headed to a campsite, well-known among overlanders—an open field next to a railway line near the center of the city. Frankly, it wasn't the most beautiful location, but it was just a hundred yards from the famous "Kano Club"—the saving grace for overland expeditions. The club was a great place to eat, drink, swim, shower and generally relax in a cool environment—essentially, it had all the material pleasures of the world. The Kano Club permitted us to buy a very cheap "temporary" membership and experience a measure of relaxation and comfort we hadn't seen in more than two months—it was like a slice of paradise! At last, we were clean most of the time, relaxed, and conscious of things other than just those necessary for survival. While I really welcomed and enjoyed the pleasures of the club, they took nothing away from the raw experience and deprivation of the desert crossing. As I sat on the patio at the Kano Club and wrote my journal, I felt compelled to portray both experiences.

During our time in Kano, John met a young local guy named Abu, who spent a lot of his time showing us around the city, helping us bargain in the markets, and inviting us to a few nightclubs with his friends.

John with Abu and friends in Kano, Nigeria

One night in particular, John and I went with Abu and a couple of his friends to a local bar in the old section of the city. Lots of people were walking along the narrow streets, which were quite dark, lit only by a few house lights and several kerosene lanterns. Taxis buzzed up and down the streets, lucky not to run over pedestrians.

Meanwhile, music blared out everywhere, people laughed and shouted to each other, and car horns honked continuously! (It was a mad house of activity) It seemed to me that African drivers took great pleasure in honking at anyone, be they on a bike, motorcycle, or in a car—each driver had one hand on the horn at all times, ready to blast a few eardrums, should the occasion arise. And of course, numerous occasions presented themselves whenever people got in the path of any vehicle. The local people were very friendly toward us, while being very curious at the same time.

Street scene in Kano, Nigeria

For John and me, it was a very different experience to be the only white folks among hundreds of black people. But it was not unfriendly in any way—in fact, it was most hospitable, something I was ashamed to say was often not true in the reverse situation. We spent the evening drinking local beer in a couple small neighborhood bars and sharing our experiences with Abu and his friends. We had a very nice time with him, and I would have liked to spend more time with him, but eventually we had to move on. It was sad to see Abu in his situation, because he was so curious about the world outside of Kano, and eager to travel. But I knew he would have little chance to do so, and maybe not a lot of hope for the future. I wanted to help him, but I had no idea how at that point.

Earlier that same day, a group of 10 people had decided to leave the expedition and travel on their own to Nairobi, rather than face more mechanical delays, as we all suspected would happen again at some point down the road. (little did any of us know at that moment just how true the suspicion would become) The contingent leaving us consisted of the folks from New York, the girls from Minnesota, and a Canadian couple. Secretly, most of us had wished a few other people, who had become a "pain in the ass" during our long trek across the desert, would have joined them. The reason they all gave for their decision to leave the trip in Kano was to get to Nairobi before Christmas and board flights back home. But for most of us who chose to remain on the trip, we felt the real reason was due to the stress and intense heat of the desert crossing, bouts of sickness, delays from mechanical breakdowns, and perhaps more importantly, the anxiety about facing another two or three months travelling overland through the heart of the Dark Continent! Instead, they all chose to buy tickets to Nairobi on Aeroflot Soviet Airlines. Although it was the cheapest airline, it would involve four stopovers, including overnight in Khartoum! (after the "split up" in Kano, I lost contact with all of them, save for the Canadian couple who would show up two months later in Tanzania)

November 7, 1974
Kano, Nigeria to Maiduguri, Nigeria

"*Farewell to the Club*" Early in the morning we left Kano, rather reluctantly, for the rigors of the road again, after having spent five days living in the lap of luxury and comfort. Kano had reassured us that once familiar things like steak, ice, cold beer, music, and news, we so often had taken for granted before the trip, still existed. Even the opportunity to shop in Kano's largest and most modern department store was a delightful experience, despite the fact that by western standards it would have been the equivalent of a small town "five and dime" store. That shopping experience gave me the strongest impression yet of how life was so "relative"!

Old market in Kano, Nigeria

As we travelled through eastern Nigeria, the grasslands, known as "elephant grass", became taller and sometimes reached the height of a man. That evening, upon entering the small town of Maiduguri, we were invited by the locals to camp in a large clearing on the edge of the town. Not long after having set up camp, the neighborhood kids showed up to watch us, as we had expected. It was obvious that we were their "entertainment" for the evening! They kept a respectful distance, but their continual pointing and laughing became annoying after some time. Meanwhile, several local ladies showed up with fresh produce and eggs for sale, which helped make dinner extra special that night.

John shopping in Maiduguri, Nigeria

November 9-12, 1974
Maiduguri, Nigeria to Ngaoundere, Cameroun

"Into a Land of Baobab Trees" The following day, we crossed the border into Cameroun, and a beautiful land of soft rolling hills covered in lush tall grass interspersed with tall Baobab trees and small shrubs.

Road through the Cameroun

The road took us up into the highlands near the border with Chad, where we encountered cooler and more humid weather—in many ways it was more pleasant. As we travelled further south and east, the tall grass became a thick carpet of green and gold, spread over the hills.

Landscape of the Cameroun

The tall Baobab trees appeared as if they were huge umbrellas bobbing on a sea of grass. Every so often we would pass through a small village of thatched huts among a small grove of trees a clearing literally "carved" out of the tall grass.

Often, people would come out of their huts, waving to us and shouting "bonjour, bonjour". And we would always do our best to return the greeting as best we could. The feeling of being in the highlands of Cameroun was very serene, peaceful, and contented.

Mother and baby in the Cameroun

As the road gained more elevation, we encountered a few mountain rain showers, which were very refreshing. Further south, we came to a high plateau where heavy clouds formed on the horizon, and as I felt the raindrops fall upon me, I suddenly became homesick for Seattle, for the first time on the trip. As the evening descended upon the land, we found a nice clearing on the edge of a small village, where we could set up camp for the night. A small local "welcoming committee" soon arrived to watch us—had our reputation for free, fun entertainment somehow proceeded us once again? As it turned out, the night was quiet, calm, cool and very pleasant.

The next morning, before leaving the village, we went to the local farmers market to stock up on fresh produce. Besides the wonderful fresh produce, we discovered the local specialty, freshly made peanut butter and chocolate. It was served on a banana leaf and eaten with the hands—it was absolutely superb! So, we bought a large bowl of chocolate and peanut butter before continuing our journey. Later that afternoon, as we drove into the heart of Cameroun, the rolling hills became more heavily forested and created a feeling of serenity and peace. In the evening, we were once again fortunate to be invited to camp in a clearing on the edge of a small village. The local villagers were very friendly and brought us some eggs and fruit for sale. It was another very pleasant night in Cameroun.

Village in the Cameroun

Late the following afternoon, as we approached the small town of Meiganga, the ghost of mechanical failures suddenly decided to pay us another visit, this time in the form of a broken rear spring assembly! We were forced to pull into a small forest clearing just off the road and set up camp for the night. This was a rare night where we had no local "audience" since we were not close to a village.

November 13-15, 1974
Meiganga, Cameroun

"An Encounter with Monsieur Gabey" The next morning, we "limped" into Meiganga to make repairs to the old bus. While Stuart and Joe went in search of a mechanic and repair shop, the rest of us took the opportunity to explore the town. It wasn't long before we discovered it to be a beautiful and friendly place. We found a nice French patisserie where we enjoyed some delicious pastries and fresh, local peanut butter while we sat on the edge of the main street among the local people. It was very relaxing and most pleasant. Quickly, the hassles of travelling began to fade away and I felt able to settle down and just enjoy the world around me. A few hours later, Stuart and Joe returned, having completed the repairs. Not far out of town, we stopped to set up camp next to a small hotel and zoo—more specifically, it was "Monsieur Gabey's" front yard! He invited us to stay and enjoy his place.

He was an eccentric old fart who had lived in Cameroun for over 40 years, after emigrating from Paris. Over the next couple of days, we found him to be quite moody—sometimes very happy and friendly, and at other times cold and unresponsive. He bordered on being an alcoholic, but he was also a gourmet chef!

Joe, Mssr Gabey, Stuart

He prepared some fabulous French dishes for us, using the fresh fruits and vegetables from his garden. Each evening, as we enjoyed dinner in his dining room, he would pick fresh mandarin oranges for dessert from a tree just outside the dining room window. Besides the delicious meals Monsieur Gabey prepared for us, he insisted we use his shower facilities very welcome relief from the hot, humid weather of central Africa!

On our last day with Monsieur Gabey, the atmosphere was a bit tense as I took a photo of him with Stuart and Joe. And as we were leaving, I had a strong feeling that he was very sad to see us go! He certainly made a strong impression on all of us, with his generous hospitality, as well as his eccentricity! Leaving Meiganga and Monsieur Gabey, we continued east toward the border with the Central African Republic (CAR). When we came to the border crossing, we encountered a series of checkpoints, all of which appeared to be the same, as well as rather meaningless. Each time we came to a checkpoint, the amount of red tape and formalities seemed so needless and petty, almost to the point of laughter. But doing so would only risk incurring the retaliation of the border officials. The whole experience was compounded by the apparent lack of order or recognition of authority.

Often, as we drove up to a small, rundown "shack" alongside the road, we would see 3 or 4 guys sitting outside, dressed in sloppy clothes, looking pretty "laid back" and quite disinterested. It was similar to several other places we had encountered on the trip. But lo and behold, this wasn't just any old rundown shack, nor were these guys just any old local "loafers". They were part of the "Grande Douane"—otherwise known as "Immigration and Customs". As we pulled to a stop beside the innocuous abode, we anxiously looked among the group of guys seated outside for someone in authority to speed us through the inevitable official "rig-a-ma-roll". Finally, out of the blue, one guy came forward to ask why we had stopped! He looked just like all the rest of them in front of the shack, but not so—he was "the" Immigration and Customs official! And so it went, from one checkpoint to another and from one country to another. The landscape never changed from one side of the border to the other, only the names on the map. As we drove into the CAR, the landscape became less mountainous and more heavily forested with taller trees. It was clear that we were now entering the edge of the "jungle" for the first time. The air became warmer and more humid the further south we went.

At the last border checkpoint, we had been informed a bridge on the main road had been washed out by recent heavy rains, so we would have to take a long detour instead. The alternate route turned out to be a very pleasant drive through a rural, less populated region of the country. The detour took us to Bouar, the country's second largest city, which wasn't saying much! From what we could see, economic development in the CAR was certainly at a pretty low level. While we were in the town, we stopped at the local farmer's market to do some shopping for fresh food. What we discovered was a fascinating collection of very diverse foods and spices being sold mostly by women, lined up in crowded rows around the town square. All of the women were dressed in an amazing array of bright colors, no two of which were dressed alike. Our cooking crew stocked up with lots of fresh fruits and vegetables, including papaya, bananas, grapefruit, peanut oil, and especially fresh peanut butter wrapped in banana leaf.

The market was a very lively and colorful place to shop, and every kid within 20 miles arrived to see the "tourists" (us)!

Halcyon with Fulani women in the market

Within a few minutes, our vehicles were surrounded by hundreds of wide-eyed children, pointing, staring, shouting, and laughing. It felt as if we were part of a parade, a sort of travelling sideshow, reminiscent of the old Barnum and Bailey Circus days! At that moment, I could almost imagine a "barker" calling out, "Step right up and see rare strange looking men from across the water. Watch them point their cameras at you, buy trinkets and souvenirs, and make funny sounds". It was truly a unique experience to be part of such an absurd "show"—at least that was how it felt from our side. But most likely, the experience for the children was just one of excitement and curiosity. And perhaps, we sometimes reacted in a similar way as we travelled through their villages. Once we had finished shopping in the market and "entertaining" the kids, we bid farewell to Buoar and continued east toward our next destination, Boali Falls.

November 16, 1974
Buoar to Boali Falls, Central African Republic

"Thunder of the Falls" We had been driving for what seemed like a long time and it was almost dark, when Stuart suddenly pulled off the main road and proceeded down a rough path to the small town of Boali Falls. Just on the other side of town was the Mbali River that tumbled into an enormous rocky gorge through a series of turbulent falls that appeared to come straight out of the forest. The waterfalls were huge, higher and wider than Niagara Falls. It was a very impressive sight, especially as the sun was setting.

Bouali Falls, Central African Republic (CAR)

It was also the site of the country's only hydro-electric power plant, part of President General Bokassa's "L-Operation Development Economique". As John and I explored the area, we found the river to be a beautiful tropical setting that provided us with a lovely place to bathe. We stripped down in the cool evening air and enjoyed a very refreshing splash in the river. It wasn't until after we got out of the river that we realized we had been a mere 20 feet from the precipice of the falls where the water tumbled down over 150 feet into the rocky gorge below! The experience was absolutely exhilarating. That night, we slept very well—relaxed from our encounter with the river.

November 17-20, 1974
Boali Falls to Bangui, Central African Republic

"Camping in the City" The next morning, John and I returned to the falls, and I took some photos in an attempt to capture the beauty and magnificence of the amazing natural phenomenon. Although I was able to take a few pictures of the falls, it was impossible to capture the roar of the rushing water and the feeling of the mist as it tumbled down into the gorge. We spent some time just sitting at the base of the falls and absorbing the sights and sounds of the surrounding forest environment. As we returned to camp, we felt it had been a very pleasant and most relaxing morning. Then we broke camp, loaded the vehicles, and headed for Banqui, the capitol city. The main road was in decent shape and we made good time, arriving early Sunday afternoon. It wasn't long before we were invited to camp on the grounds of the "Centre Protestante du Jeaunesse", a French mission school for young boys, a couple of miles from the city center. It was a religious school to prepare young local boys for university in France. They lived at the school and had to study quite hard in order to be admitted into university.

We set up camp in a very nice courtyard behind the mission. We had access to the facilities in the mission, including wonderful showers, a place to wash clothes, and toilets of the "real kind". Because of the very warm, humid weather, the showers were most welcome. As we explored Bangui over the next few days, we found it to be a pretty modern city, with lots of stores and large street markets, where most of the local people shopped. And for the first time, we began to see lots of ivory carvings for sale. They were beautiful but very expensive, as expected. As a matter of fact, virtually everything that was imported was outrageously priced—a small tin of peaches sold for 350 CFA, or about $1.50!

"Catching Grasshoppers on a Sunday Night" In search of an evening's

entertainment, four of us headed down the street toward a local bar for a couple of beers. As we approached an intersection, a large crowd of young kids was milling around under the bright streetlamps, catching grasshoppers.

Catching grasshoppers in Bangui, CAR

As we walked through the crowd, they began to stare and laugh at us, and a few threw stones. It quickly became a rather ugly scene, especially for the two girls in our group. Finally, some older boys stepped in and stopped the younger kids from throwing stones, which was much appreciated! This sort of thing had happened to us a few times before, with young kids throwing rocks at our vehicles as we passed through a village. I attributed it to the case of each kid trying to "show off" and prove his strength in front of the group, but it could easily get out of hand. So, although having weathered the adversity, we still felt a bit apprehensive about continuing to walk down the street. However, the older boys were kind enough to escort us to the bar, where people were dancing to the sounds of James Brown.

Once inside the open courtyard of the bar, we sat down, ordered cold beers, and watched the local people dancing. Once again, we were the only white folks among the crowd. Besides the people in the bar, there was a large crowd standing just outside, watching the dancing and listening to the music. Then suddenly, out of the dark night sky came a horde of grasshoppers, attracted to the bright lights of the bar. Immediately, everyone stopped dancing and began grabbing the grasshoppers—putting them in bottles or stringing them on long twigs. It was really a wild scene, with people picking up grasshoppers from the tables, snatching them out of the air, and even grabbing them from people's hair!

Meanwhile, the music continued to blare out of an old, dilapidated loudspeaker from a scratchy old record. We found the local people in the bar to be great! Many of them invited us to dance and taught us the "right" way to move to the African rhythm. They were having a wonderful time and really wanted us to have a marvelous evening as well. They were very nice, warm, friendly people—always laughing, sometimes with us and other times at us. But we must have looked funny at times. The evening turned out to be a beautiful and enjoyable one, despite a rather shaky beginning!

November 20-21, 1974
Bangui, Central African Republic

"Biding our Time in Bangui" Our time in Bangui was extending beyond the original schedule, due to the need to apply for new visas to enter Zaire. Our original visas had expired many days before, a result of the long delays we had encountered in the Sahara. The formalities and bureaucracy within the Zaire government had forced us to stay a few more days in Bangui. But in all honesty, it was a very pleasant place to be stuck, although an expensive one. We were able to enjoy a few great meals in a couple of marvelous French restaurants, as well as morning pastries from the local patisserie. However, our finances limited the dining experiences to a couple of evenings, before we had to retreat to the bland, dehydrated camp food!

During our time in Bangui, the presence of the President, General Bokassa, was literally everywhere. The vast majority of public works and government buildings were named in his honor. In addition, the presence of the military was clearly evident, with lots of soldiers on the streets, and army vehicles constantly on the move. Despite this, we felt no pressure upon us as tourists. However, it was abundantly evident that it was a military dictatorship, openly displayed in the capitol city. We saw many impressive new government buildings, which led me to believe General Bokassa was putting all of the country's wealth into developing his hometown, Bangui.

On one day, he came out of his Presidential Palace in a huge motorcade of at least a dozen police cars and 50 motorcycles, all with their sirens screaming, whizzing madly through the center of the city. My first guess was it must have been "staged" to impress the local people with his power. I also suspected the length of the motorcade and number of motorcycles must have been proportional to the stature of the government official! One afternoon, as John and I sat on the terrace of the New Palace Hotel enjoying a cold beer, overlooking the central square downtown,

New Palace Hotel, Bangui, CAR

we saw the makings of a classic Humphrey Bogart film, set in downtown Bangui. We figured the story line would go something like:

"It was nearly noon, and activity in Bangui was rapidly grinding to a halt. The slightest bit of a breeze had disappeared, along with most of the people, as they scurried off to their afternoon siestas. The big wheel of the ceiling fan in the bar slowly turned, desperately trying to stave off the intense heat of the tropical sun. The day slowly slipped into the afternoon, almost as slowly as the sun fell toward the sunset. Suddenly, the scream of several sirens broke the sullen silence, as two dozen police cars raced toward the central square, and quickly turned in the direction of the New Palace Hotel. Just as swiftly, police officers dashed up the hotel steps, hurtled the terrace railing, and pounced on a man dressed in a fur-lined trench coat, wearing dark glasses and a white panama hat. They dragged him to a waiting black limousine, as he screamed for mercy. With tires smoking and sirens blaring, they made their way to the Presidential Palace at the far end of the boulevard. Throughout the whole episode, we sat quietly at our table, sipping our martinis, just as we had seen Humphrey do so many times!"

November 22-23, 1974
Bangui to Bambari, Central African Republic

"I Feel like a Parade" Finally, the day came when we received our new visas for Zaire. As we packed up our tents and loaded our gear on the vehicles, we bade a fond farewell to Bangui and set out for unknown destinations in Zaire. Our route from Bangui took us east through a very rural region of CAR, past clearing after clearing in the dense forest and thick grassland. Each small clearing held a collection of grass and mud huts in the form of a village. Each time, as we rumbled past in a cloud of red dust, the sleepy villages came to life, and people peered at us from every corner and doorway. At first, they would stare with a strange, curious, inquisitive look that seemed to yearn for some measure of acknowledgement and recognition. In response, I felt the urge to wave a greeting to them. And I found, almost as quickly as I raised my arm, they also did the same, with as much or more fervor. It made me feel

61

very good to see the warmth and sincerity of their smiles. The response of the young kids was even more so—their awe and amazement at the sight of us had them jumping and shouting to us, all the time waving, their whole-body wriggling! It was always fun to watch them village after village. Even for the briefest of moments, I felt as if, in some small way, I had met them and understood something about their life, and perhaps even a glimpse of their future. Then I wondered, what did they feel or understand from our brief encounter? Sadly, at that moment, I knew I would never find out.

But, after 8 hours of continuous encounters with the people in the small villages, my arm became tired, my mind began to dull my expression, and my thoughts drifted to other things. It was at that time, the villages started to become the same, the people began to look the same, and even the days became the same. But for the villagers, it was a new "parade" every time we passed. In reality, it was the local people who were different and we who were the same. I came to believe, for each village, we were really like a parade passing in review, our vehicles were the "floats", and we were the "beauty queens" waving to the crowd. And late in the day, when my arm tired, the wave became a "mechanical" one, as my thoughts drifted miles away. It was then that I felt I was indeed part of a parade. That evening, we stopped at a repair shop and junk yard just outside the small town of Bambari, to have some welding done on the old bus. Once it was completed, the shop owner invited us to camp next door. The campsite was certainly welcome, though it was also one of the strangest places we had camped on the trip. That night it felt a bit weird as we sat around the campfire, surrounded by the wreckage of many vehicles casting eerie shadows in the night. I couldn't help wondering how many ghosts were roaming around the wrecking yard that night!

November 24, 1974
Bambari to Moyabe, Central African Republic

"Camping in the Jungle" Early the next morning, we left Bambari and the junk yard. Most of the day was spent slowly climbing to the summit of an extensive volcanic plateau, where the landscape changed from dense forest to rolling hills of tall grass savannah. It was also a region of large coffee and banana plantations dotting the hills in a patchwork of lush fields. It felt good to be at a higher elevation and able to see the whole countryside. And all the time, the beautiful scenery was passing by, and my hand was constantly waving in response to the great numbers of people excited to greet us in every little village along the way.

Passing through a village in CAR

(the "parade" moved on to new villages and towns every day!) Late in the afternoon, as we neared the Oubangui River and the border with Zaire, we came to the top of an escarpment overlooking a massive ribbon of water slowly making its way downriver, between dark green hills on either side. The view was spectacular from our high vantage point.

After a few photographs, we made our way down a narrow, twisting dirt road to the small river town of Moyabe. The town was situated on the banks of the river, framed by high hills on one side and rushing rapids on the other. As we pulled into the small town, I could see tall palm trees lining the streets, and remnants of some old French colonial houses along the river's edge. Just as we parked near the center of town, an intense tropical thunderstorm loomed overhead. Within minutes, there was a mighty crash of thunder and heavy rain poured down upon us. Though it lasted only 15–20 minutes, the hard wind driven rain broke the lazy, sleepy spell of the afternoon like the roar of a lion! In the aftermath of the storm, the air became cool and sparkling—the effect was both refreshing and exhilarating, much like a cold shower in the morning. The pleasant feeling carried on into the evening and made it a wonderful night for sleeping beside the river. Meanwhile, I sat on the shore and watched the local people go about their daily life, piloting their dugout canoes, known as "pirouettes," up and down the river.

Pirouette on the Oubangui River, CAR

Chapter five

November 25, 1974
Moyabe, Central African Republic to Banzyville,
Zaire

"*Into the Heart of The Dark Continent* " The next morning, as I arose with the sun, I looked upon a scene that could have easily been lifted from a James Michener novel—local fishermen in their dugout canoes glided smoothly on the still waters of the river, and the fog slowly vanished as the sun rose over the distant hills. We made ready to cross the river on another small ferry, but there was a bit of a hassle with the ferry boat captain who tried to charge us three times the rate set by the government. After some discussion with him, we finally boarded the ferry to Zaire. The voyage across the massive river was unique. At the beginning, the pilot headed upstream in the calm water, then he pointed the boat into the strong current in the middle of the river and drifted downstream. Slowly he steered the ferry toward the opposite shore.

Once we had docked, we immediately encountered the Zaire government Immigration and Customs officials. They conducted a very thorough search of our gear. Stuart decided to have us stow our cameras in a locked storage compartment, due to the very strict government regulations restricting photographs within the country. Reluctantly, we surrendered our cameras. It was unfortunate that we couldn't rely on the common sense of a few people in our group to know when it was not appropriate to take a photograph. As a result, I was unable to take any photos for almost two weeks during our journey through Zaire—very unfortunate! In addition to the very thorough search of our gear, there was some hassle about the government's requirement that tourists entering the country had to show sufficient funds of $40.00 USD per day while travelling through Zaire. Our understanding from other overland groups was that the requirement was rarely enforced, but this particular official was intent upon exercising his authority.

As it turned out, he was so stupid in his calculations of how much money we would need as a group to meet the $40.00 USD per day per person, he divided by 4 instead of multiplying, as he should have! So, the first few members of our group easily satisfied the requirement and we were allowed entry into Zaire. And after more than 4 hours waiting, with a great deal of patience, we finally rolled on down the road and found a nice spot to camp for the night just outside the village of Banzyville. Later that evening, the village locals turned out to help us pitch our tents, and then came back with fresh fruits, vegetables, and eggs for sale. It seemed as if we always managed to draw a large "audience" wherever we went. And it was always "standing room only" for our nightly performances—and that night was no exception! By this point during our journey, we had gotten accustomed to doing almost everything in front of a crowd! (at that moment, I had the thought—"what would I do if I didn't have someone watching me?") A few of us discovered an abandoned hut nearby for a quiet, restful sleep.

November 27, 1974
Banzyville, Zaire to Bumba, Zaire

"It was Someone who just Looked Like Me" We began the day as the sun rose, packed up our gear, and headed down the road, deeper into the jungle. Having passed so many laughing, smiling, friendly faces for days on end, it was a real shock when we began encountering some negative reactions from people as we passed through their villages and proceeded south toward Bumba. It started with young kids shouting "tourist" and

throwing rocks at our vehicles. Later, in a few of the villages, older people shook their fists and waved knives in the air! As the day wore on and we passed through a couple of small towns, the negative reactions became more common. While none of us were directly threatened, our feeling was one of sadness and frustration.

As I recalled the recent history of the region, I began to suspect the reason for the negative feeling we were witnessing might well have to do with the recent "War of Liberation", when the colonial government had been overthrown. We were travelling through the heart of the former "Belgian Congo", where a strong colonial power had held almost iron rule for decades. It had been a white supremacist system of government that held a vast majority of the local population in a state of servitude. When independence finally came, it had come with a vengeance and much bloodshed. Being that only 10 years had passed since then, it was no wonder that many local people remained bitter toward whites.

That's when I realized, many of the women who screamed at us and shook their fists, must have lost a husband, son, or brother in the war against the Belgians. And the expressions on the faces of many of the young men I saw, painted a perfect portrait of "angry young men". While all of the negative feelings seemed to be directed at me, as a symbol of the evils and transgressions of the old colonial system, I yearned to tell these people who cursed and shook their fists at me, "it wasn't me, it was someone who just looked like me"! But there was neither the time nor place to sit down and discuss it with them. The experience that day forced me to withdraw into my own world and be much more reserved in my interaction with the local people. I felt a bit sad in doing so, but it was in self-defense to keep from being hurt personally by the insults hurled at me, or more accurately, at what I "represented". At days end, I began looking forward to leaving Zaire, unfortunately.

That evening, we camped on the grounds of an old plantation house that had been abandoned by its former Belgian owner and taken over by the local village chief. He was kind enough to let us camp in his "front yard". Just as we began to set up camp, some Louisiana boys came by, driving an old "International Travelall". They stopped and shared our campsite. Over dinner that evening, they told us about a new route up the Zaire River, once known as the Congo River. But the route would involve crossing the river three times.

November 28-29, 1974
Bumba, Zaire to Basoko, Zaire

"Congo Crossing" The next morning, we bade farewell to the village chief and the Louisiana boys, then headed for our meeting with the river. When we arrived at the first crossing, we were told it would be a long ferry ride, so we hoped to get both vehicles on at the same time. But the ferry captain wouldn't have it that way, So, we lost a full half day making two trips! There were many small islands in the middle of the river, which made it difficult to fully appreciate the extent of it until we boarded the ferry. The trip across the mighty river was incredible, as the ferry snaked its way among the islands. The river was very wide, muddy, and slow moving—much the same as I remembered of the Mississippi River in southern Louisiana. The river crossing was awesome—one of the largest rivers in the world. At one point, as we approached the middle of the river, the view was more like that of a huge lake or ocean bay. With the abundance of palm trees and overhanging vines along the shore, I felt I was definitely in the tropical jungle. As the ferry continued across the river, we began seeing a lot of dugout canoes carrying people and their goods to market. Gazing upon the scene, I began to imagine we had become part of the classic film, "The African Queen"—and I even wondered if we might see Humphrey Bogart!

Due to the numerous islands in the river, the ferry crossing took over an hour to reach the far shore. Once we were safely on the other side of the river, we found a small crowd of locals gathered around a Land Rover with a flat tire. The driver seemed quite perplexed, since he had no tire wrench or even a jack - quite a shaky situation in the middle of Zaire! So, Stuart organized a crew of us to solve the problem. Some of our group grabbed a long pole from the forest and levered up the vehicle, while Stuart and I changed the flat tire. It was rather a comical scene the locals cheered us on as we stood on the long pole holding up the Land Rover. Later in the afternoon, we drove up the hill to await the arrival of our truck. As we sat beside the road in the shade of the forest, a kind old lady came along and gave us fresh lemons and papaya from the trees in her front yard. Her gift was very much appreciated, and I began to feel much better about being in Zaire!

November 30, 1974
Basoko, Zaire to Elizabetha, Zaire

"Remains of a Colonial Empire" After having crossed the river, we encountered very friendly local people once again, in contrast to our negative experience in the past couple of days. During the next few hours, we passed through several abandoned small towns and plantations that appeared to be so noticeably "westernized", once part of a great colonial empire. There were dilapidated buildings and empty fields everywhere. They almost resembled old ghost towns of the American West. The luster and prosperity had left with their former European owners. Now only a ghostly shell remained—a sad scene to witness. It was the result of the process of "nationalization" by the Zaire government, following the end of the "war of liberation" and the expulsion of Belgians. Some of the houses and buildings had been taken over by local people, but it was pretty obvious they took less interest in upkeeping maintenance than the former European owners. I hoped that perhaps someday the local people would return them to their former glory.

As evening approached, we came to the small town of Elizabetha, an old cocoa and palm plantation managed by the Zaire government following nationalization. The town had suffered much the same fate as other places in the region—abandoned buildings with crumbled plaster and rusted iron from years of neglect. We were fortunate that evening to find an Episcopal mission that invited us to camp for the night. And as usual, there were a hundred curious, sometimes suspicious pairs of eyes forming a perimeter around our campsite. At first it seemed OK, but as the evening dragged on, the kids got more rambunctious and louder. Finally, some adults came and quickly shooed them away, much to our relief. And to our delight, the mission had toilets (the proper "sit down" type) and showers, which made for a welcome change from the mud and grease of the past few days. The mission was kind enough to let us stay a second night in order for us to replace a broken front spring and complete some minor repairs on the bus. We left on Sunday morning to the sound of children singing in the chapel.

December 1, 1974
Elizabetha, Zaire to Isangi, Zaire

"The Funeral" or "Hail to the Chief" It felt good to be back on the road again, but the feeling wasn't destined to last very long. Just a few miles down the muddy dirt road, Kong slipped off the edge and into a deep ditch. The road was very narrow and ran through a large swampy region, making the edge of the road very soft, almost like quicksand, although it was not so obvious. Our best chance was to use the truck to pull the old girl back out of the mudhole. We spent a couple of hours wallowing in the thick red mud and a lot of sweat before the bus was able to escape the ditch and return to the road. However, the joy of our success was tempered by the discovery that one of the front spring assemblies on the bus had broken during the process! At that point we decided to press on to Isangi, the next closest town, for repairs. But further along the road we entered a small village and were immediately surrounded by a large crowd of people laughing and dancing to the loud, pulsating beat of a jungle drum—a hollowed out tree trunk. The whole village seemed to be celebrating an important event, and most people were dressed in native costume for a gala party.

We stopped to find out what was going on, and several of the local people told us it was a ceremony to honor the old village chief who had died a few days before, and to celebrate the new village chief.

Funeral celebration in Zaire

Immediately we were invited to join the celebration, yet we still had repairs to make. What to do— there was a great deal of confusion and commotion about how to deal with the situation—whether to press on or stay? Stuart, Dave and I decided to move down the road a couple of hundred yards and do a quick replacement of the spring assembly, no doubt a new record time! Meanwhile, the rest of our group quickly became caught up in the festivities.

Once the repairs had been completed, the three of us were invited to join in the celebration. It wasn't long before many of the villagers dragged us into the midst of the dancing, and soon we were all doing our best to keep up with them, even though we didn't have much experience dancing to the rhythm of the drums. The men of the village danced within an inner circle, while carrying tall spears. And in the center of the circle, the big drum was being beaten by half a dozen guys. The whole village was pulsating with the strong beat as it echoed throughout the surrounding jungle. Several of us were invited into the house of the new chief to share his homemade beer. As we were leaving, he gave us a huge basket of pineapple and cassava as a departing gift.

But before leaving the village, a couple of the old men asked us to take their photos as they posed in their ceremonial costumes—a rare thing in Zaire, since photos were so often restricted or even forbidden! The whole experience was so unexpected, and upon reflection, I felt more like I was part of a National Geographic documentary film. But it was for real and became one of my most memorable moments. Later that evening, on the outskirts of Isangi, we were invited to camp on the front lawn of a primary school. And once again, we found ourselves surrounded by a throng of kids, obviously fascinated by the sudden sight of strange visitors!

December 2, 1974
Isangi, Zaire to Yangambi, Zaire

"Tires in the Mud" or *"Rubber in the Muck"* The next morning, we left Isangi and crossed the Zaire River once again. This time the ferry was able to take both vehicles at the same time for the one-hour trip. It was a pleasant ride across the huge river, but once we reached the far shore, we soon discovered a long stretch of road that harbored one of the worst mud holes in all of Zaire—a country well known for some of the worst roads in the world! As we departed the ferry, we met another overland group from Nairobi headed west to Kisangani. They gave us some bad news about having been stuck in a monstrous mud hole for two days about 2 miles up the road. So, we prepared for the worst and headed for our meeting with the mud. As we came over a small hill, we saw an old African truck already stuck up to its axles in the thick red clay. And even though it had 4-wheel drive, it was unable to pull itself free of the giant mud hole. The truck driver begged us to pull him out so he could try again. But by this time in our journey we were wise to the troubles of mud.

So, we decided to have lunch and think things through. As we ate our tinned meat and crackers, we discussed the idea of constructing an alternate route around the mud hole and the truck stuck in it. Having finished lunch, Stuart and Joe organized our group into a "road building crew". Everyone pitched in by cutting wood, filling smaller mud holes, and draining muddy water off the road. Our new route was finished in a couple of hours, and although it was only 100 feet in length, it was enough to avoid the bottomless pit of muck that had trapped other vehicles. We must have been a real sight to behold for the locals as they watched us wallowing around half naked in the thick red mud! But we did a fine job of hasty road construction and were able to get our two vehicles past the monster mud hole. We were also able to pull out the old African truck as well and send it on its way.

"Road building" in Zaire

Alas, our triumph was short lived as we rolled up to another large mud hole, less than a mile up the road. It was filled with water and looked to be quite deep. A couple of cars made it through with some difficulty, but as Stuart guided Kong through the muck, it slipped off the main track and the rear end fell into a deep hole! Suddenly, the entire front end of the old bus rose into the air at an awkward angle—the front wheels being entirely off the ground.

King Kong stuck in a mud hole, Zaire

King Kong "stuck"!

We got out of the bus as best as we could, and then everyone began taking photos of the old girl. We started discussing options for getting the vehicle out of the mud hole. As Joe was hooking up the tow chain from the truck to pull the bus out backwards, an old Volkswagen bug came screaming through the tall grass on the side of the road, trying to get around us. There was nothing but deep mud on either side of the road, however, that did not deter the driver from trying to "bully" his way through the muck! And as everyone expected, the little car soon sank up to its axles.

Then, out of the blue, about a dozen locals literally picked up the car and practically carried it through the knee-deep mud. It was an incredible sight to watch as they all chanted in rhythm to coordinate their efforts. Throughout our journey through the jungle, whenever we had been stuck, or someone else was, the first response of the locals was always one of brute force—just push, no matter how deep the mud! Sometimes it worked and other times not—but there was never a lack of energy or enthusiasm when it came to pushing.

Finally, Joe was able to pull Kong out of the mud hole, and Stuart deftly "skirted" it to continue on our way. As evening approached, we were invited to stay at another Catholic mission in the small town of Yangambi. As we began setting up camp, we were once again surrounded by an "audience" of young children, eager to watch our every move. As the evening went on, they grew more excited and noisier. About two hours later, some local police arrived and drove them away—rather roughly and perhaps uncalled for. The next day, we explored the old town, a former Belgian rubber plantation that once thrived, as could be seen by many old vacant buildings. There was an old Shell service station, an abandoned auto repair garage, and a classic old European hotel downtown, now vacant and slowly fading away. The town had just a faint "glimmer" of its elegant past, revealed beneath the dust and crumbling concrete. Again, as I looked around, the scene was so reminiscent of an old ghost town from the American West. The whole experience was fascinating, and yet a bit sad at the same time. Who knows if the town would ever recover its former glory?

Local market "entertainer" in Zaire

December 3, 1974

Yangambi, Zaire to Kisangani, Zaire (formerly Stanleyville)

"In the Shadow of Dr. Livingstone" Early the next morning, we broke camp and left the mission in Yangambi. Later, we encountered yet another crossing of the mighty Zaire River on a small ferry just west of Kisangani. (the local Kikongo name for Stanleyville, the former capitol of the Belgian Congo As we drove along a newly improved road on the far side of the river, the engine in the old bus suddenly sputtered and then died in the middle of the road! It looked like the ghost of mechanical failures had caught up with us again, a mere 10 kms from the city. It didn't take long to find the problem—lack of fuel! Having travelled over 6 weeks without receiving any mail since Kano, we were all anxious to find lots of mail from family and friends awaiting us in Kisangani. So, Stuart went ahead with Joe in the truck to collect mail before the post office closed. A couple hours later, with a fresh supply of

diesel fuel, we limped into the city. Unfortunately, we found very little mail since there hadn't been enough time to forward it from London. So, we would have to wait until we got to Rwanda to pick up loads of mail, or so we all hoped!

However, all was not lost—we found Kisangani to be quite a modern city, though not large by European or American standards. We availed ourselves of the opportunity to browse the shops and partake of the delicacies of a French pastry shop. As we walked the streets we found the local people to be very friendly and helpful, in contrast to some of the expectations we had at the beginning of our entry into the country—since the ravages of the war of independence from Belgium had ended only a few short years before. It even appeared that a few of the former Belgian owners had returned to invest in the local economy after the war. After doing some shopping for essential provisions we would need for the next leg of our journey through the remote jungle of eastern Zaire, we headed to a campground on the shore of the river a few kms north of the city and downstream from Stanley Falls.

What we discovered was a beautiful site with a lovely sandy beach, lots of tall palm trees, and several grass covered huts. It was a very pleasant place to setup camp, having beautiful views of the river and the waterfall! And a short time later, we would learn that we had camped directly below the city zoo on the embankment above us! That evening, John showed up, following his 3-day journey up the Zaire River from Isangi to Kisangani by boat. He had many stories to share about the boat trip, and he was excited to hear about our adventures on the road during his sojourn. So, it was a very enjoyable evening of storytelling around the campfire.

December 4, 1974
Kisangani, Zaire

"Passing Time at the Bank" or *"What's the Holdup?"* The next morning, thinking we would be leaving Kisangani that afternoon, (we should have known better by now) a small group of us headed straight to the bank to change money for the rest of the trip through Zaire. This was the story, as it happened!

The Place: "Banque Nationale du Zaire"—a huge old stone building on the main city square, surrounded by a high steel fence topped with barbed wire

The Time: 9:00 am—opening of the bank

The People: Six tourists (us) and 14 bank officials

Upon entering the bank lobby, we waited for someone to notice us and offer some assistance—that was mistake #1. After 15 minutes of being ignored by the bank staff, Halcyon took the lead and cornered a man sitting behind a desk. He finally gave us several forms to fill out, including Customs Declarations, and what was to eventually become a staggering amount of red tape and clumsy bureaucracy. Papers were passed from one desk to another, as new forms were typed in quadruplicate—over and over again!

Hours passed, as it seemed to us, and the large clock on the wall confirmed it as well. The bank officials continued to shuffle papers with a distinct lack of progress, almost to the point of absurdity, even bordering on insanity! After waiting more than 3 hours, the gigantic hoax that had been perpetrated upon us finally came to an end, and our traveler's checks were cashed at last. The final straw came when we were told the bank had closed an hour earlier, and we had to be let out by the security guards! As we stood outside the bank, we all agreed the experience had been unreal, and most definitely had won the "Royal Red Tape Award" for the lack of efficiency or progress toward becoming a bank. We spent the afternoon shopping at the local farmer's market for produce and fruit to supplement our dehydrated rations on the long journey ahead through the jungle. Back in camp that evening, we shared our story of the bank with the rest of our group, which by that time had taken on a more hilarious perspective.

December 5, 1974
Kisangani, Zaire

"The Last Loo Stop" or *"Will We Ever Meet Again?"* As we prepared to break camp the next morning, we discovered several more mechanical problems with the old bus, and our time in Kisangani was seen to be stretching out far beyond our original expectations. In previous group discussions, there had been a plan to split up the two vehicles upon reaching Goma or perhaps Rwanda, in order for some of the members of the group to get to Nairobi for flights back to London before Christmas. But given the new problems with the bus, it was decided to revise the plan and split up in Kisangani the next morning. The afternoon was spent loading the truck with the gear of the rest of the "New Yorkers", the "Kiwis", and a half dozen "Aussies" who had flights booked from Nairobi. As we all sat down to dinner around the campfire that evening, there was a lot of last-minute conversation, possibly for the last time, with friends who would be leaving us, after having spent the past four months travelling together from Morocco to Zaire.

After dinner, there was a mad rush to get everything in order for an early morning departure of the truck. It was amidst this atmosphere of farewells, the now famous "Loo Group" made their last trek together into the bush for their mysterious toilet rites, a ceremony which very few had witnessed. So, it was impossible to describe the event. As the Loo Group gathered in the center of camp, they chatted some small talk in preparation for their last walk together. An obvious note of sadness filled the air as they slowly headed toward the bush, shovel in hand and "bum rolls" at the ready for their final rendezvous with nature!

As they moved into the shadowy darkness, voices choked on words of reminiscence and fond farewell— but there was also a touch of bravado about the future. Somehow, we all knew they would manage, though it wasn't immediately clear to us or them. And although they were now divided in ranks, they were as strong as ever. To those of us in camp, it was a most inspiring moment—a fitting example of courage in the face of uncertainty. (We should all take note from this experience, for there is a lesson for each of us as we take our own personal "loo stops"!) So, we said thanks to the Loo Group for their many "inspiring" moments throughout the trip, and we'll surely miss the sight of shovel and bums in line!

December 6, 1974
Kisangani, Zaire

"It's all Happening at the Zoo" The following morning, the truck pulled out of the campground, bound for Nairobi. For the rest of us, we were now alone with King Kong and on our own for the first time. Our campsite on the river, surrounded by thick forest, was a lovely place to begin repairs to the old bus, which would take us a couple more days. It wasn't long before some of us discovered that not only was the city Zoo on the hill above our camp, there was also a plush nightclub next door to the zoo, appropriately named "The Zoo". One evening, a few of our group decided to check it out, and made their way up the hill to The Zoo for a cold beer and to listen to the music. As it turned out, the place was an elegant bar and restaurant, filled with local people, mostly well dressed, quietly drinking beer and listening to the easy rhythm of a local band.

Earlier that evening, Marion and I had been invited to a barbeque on the beach by members of the Zaire River Expedition who were camped nearby. The expedition was composed of British Army officers, soldiers from the Zaire Army, and researchers from various universities and scientific organizations from around the world. Both of us were treated like royalty, and stuffed to the gills with all manner steak, sausages, bacon, and all the beer we could drink—a marvelous experience, especially after months of having nothing but dehydrated foods! Later in the evening they insisted that we join them for drinks at the "Club" (aka "The Zoo") There were 150 men and only 8 women on the expedition, which meant that Marion's time was almost always occupied by conversation with at least 3 guys at the same time.

During the evening, we met a British Colonel who had commanded an Indian Gurkha regiment on a previous expedition through the Darian Gap, between Colombia and Panama. Meanwhile, activity at The Zoo was beginning to heat up, when suddenly, some members of the westbound SIAFU overland group showed up. Apparently, they had just travelled through Uganda and been treated royally by the country's president, "Big Daddy Amin"! As the local band played some very fine, mellow songs, we all danced outside on the terrace under the stars, surrounded by tall palm trees. It was truly an idyllic setting, overlooking the river at night, with lights illuminating the waterfalls.

As the night progressed, a few members of the Zaire River Expedition decided to take over the band's guitars and drums during a break, and then proceeded to crank out some great, classic 50's rock-n-roll! The locals were amazed and delighted—they all thought it was a gas, especially to see all of us dancing to the music. Needless to say, we enjoyed a fantastic evening, more than amply supplied with free local "Primus" beer, the major national sponsor of the expedition. It was certainly a night to remember, as well as, a pleasant "diversion" from the overland travel routine.

December 7 - 9, 1974
Kisangani, Zaire to Bafwasende, Zaire

"Night of the Red Mud" After a long delay the following morning, trying to get the old bus fueled and, on our way, we made a short stop at the French patisserie for the last time, and then headed east out of the city. Stuart wanted to press ahead and do some "night driving" with Dave to make up lost time. Though we hated to leave the lovely campsite, we were anxious to continue our journey. All seemed to be going well as a much smaller group, and a certain feeling of closeness seemed to be developing among us for the first time. But as luck would have it, all was too good to be true. Just as darkness fell upon us, rounding a curve, we came to a most bizarre, absurd scene. There in the middle of the road was a truck stuck in thick, sticky red mud.

As we approached in the darkness, we heard a lot of shouting and commotion from what seemed like a hundred people. In reality, it was a Zaire Army truck stuck in the mud, with over 30 soldiers milling around aimlessly, some of whom were obviously stoned. A few of them were trying to push the truck, while most just stood around talking and laughing! It was a real leaderless bunch, so Stuart and John used their fluency in French to organize the army troops and some of our people to push the truck out of the mud. Not only was the truck stuck helplessly in the mud, its battery was dead! After some time hassling with the soldiers, we were able to get everyone pushing at the same time in the same direction. Finally, after a couple of hours, we managed to get them on their way.

But success was once again short-lived—no sooner had they disappeared down the road, than we became stuck in the middle of the road. This time it wasn't the red mud that brought us to a halt, it was a blocked fuel line. After several attempts to get the bus moving again, all of which were unsuccessful, we were graciously pulled back out of the mud hole by a couple of African trucks who then promptly shot past us into the night! So, with no other options, we spent the rest of the night camped on the road in the middle of the red mud.

Camped on the road in Zaire

Stuart, Dave and I spent the better part of the next day fixing the fuel line problem, while the rest of our group sat patiently on the side of the road in the heat of the jungle. By late afternoon, we had the fuel line problem solved and were back on the road for another attempt of night driving. It was just a few miles down the road when the "ghost" suddenly reared its ugly head again and blocked the fuel line once more! By this time, darkness had fallen on the jungle, so we had no choice but to spend another night camped in the middle of the road. As we sat around the campfire that night, Stuart, Dave, and I expressed our frustration with the continuous mechanical problems and unsuccessful attempts to do some night driving to make up lost time. As Stuart put it quite well, and in plain language, "it seems we just can't get our shit together"! Both Dave and I responded with, "maybe someday we will".

Early the next morning, John was off on another sojourn, hitching a ride with an old African truck bound for Komanda, deep in the Ituri forest of eastern Zaire, and a large plantation owned by a Pakistani man who he had met while we were camped in Kisangani. Meanwhile, Stuart, Dave and I spent a couple of hours dealing with the fuel line problem again. At last we were able to get the old girl running, but success was once again short lived when the ghost played another dastardly trick on us. Incredibly, just 10 miles down the road, the clutch pedal broke—something that should never happen! Fortunately, Stuart was able to "grind" the gears until we limped into the Pakistani plantation.

As we pulled off the road, John greeted us and we were invited to a beautiful lunch as guests of the Pakistani plantation owner. (Once again, John came through with an amazing feat of advance public relations! Later that afternoon, we drove a couple of miles down the road to camp in an abandoned gravel quarry, where the Zaire River Expedition had set up their camp as well. It was great to meet up with them again, and they showed us some of their animal traps and survey equipment. We shared dinner with them around the campfire that evening, and it was a delightful time of fascinating conversation and storytelling. Before retiring for the night, a few of us took the opportunity to bathe in the rushing rapids of a tropical stream nearby—a most refreshing experience!

December 10 - 11, 1974
Bafwasende, Zaire to Station de l'Epulu, Zaire

"A Meeting with the Pygmies" The next morning, we drove back to the plantation, where we were able to make some temporary repairs to the broken clutch pedal. After the repairs were completed, the Pakistani owner insisted that we stay for breakfast, an elaborate buffet we could hardly refuse. Then we were back on the road with full stomachs and light hearts! However, the "jerry-rigged" clutch pedal soon gave out and Stuart was back to grinding gears. We were headed to the next major town, Station de l'Epulu", where Stuart had been told there might be some Bedford truck parts, which would be of great help in making repairs to the old bus. As we made our way through the jungle, we were entering the Ituri Forest, a region dominated by the Pygmy people.

Less than half an hour later, as we were slowly passing through a small village, heavy rain began to fall, so typical of the almost daily tropical showers we had experienced throughout Zaire. As we slowed to a stop, we were suddenly surrounded by people running out of their huts and from under trees, carrying all manner of things to trade with us. Soon we were in the middle of a crowd of smiling Pygmies, shouting to us and wanting to trade bows and arrows, baskets, hash pipes, and wood carvings for our old T-Shirts, empty custard tins, and even John's "Binaca breath mints"! It was a crazy scene to see all the Pygmies standing in the drenching rain and having a ball trading with us. They were truly beautiful and jovial people!

At one point, a woman came running out of a hut with a basket to trade, when suddenly her husband saw her and "shooed" her back into their hut, scolding her for trying to trade their basket. We all got a chuckle out of it! Just as we were about to leave the village, an old man came shuffling toward us with another bow and arrow set to trade, just like everyone else. But this little old man had such a beautiful smile and turned up face, that he couldn't help making us all laugh and smile. There he was, hurrying toward us at a snail's pace, but as fast as he could run—it was a special scene that stayed with me. Leaving the village was a bit sad as we knew we would never have the opportunity to experience such a wonderful feeling with these people again.

As we came to Station de l'Epulu, we were invited to take a short tour of their zoo. The highlight was an encounter with the elusive "Okapi", a native animal of the Ituri Forest.

"Okapi" - Station d'Epulu, Ituri Forest, Zaire

It was a strange cross between a giraffe and a zebra—a beautiful animal and quite shy. That evening, several miles down the road, we found another abandoned gravel quarry for our campsite. It was alongside a small river that afforded us another opportunity to take a cool, refreshing bath before retiring for the night. It was a most delightful evening in the heart of the Ituri Forest.

December 12, 1974
Komanda, Zaire

"Coming Out of the Jungle" As I looked at the Michelin map of Africa before we left camp the next morning, there was a large green colored area that represented dense forest, in other words, jungle. There was also a long straight line where the green area stopped and a light brown area began, representing grassland. Of course, in reality on the ground, there could be no straight line or abrupt change from jungle to grassland— or could there be? Near the village of Komanda we encountered such a strange phenomenon of nature that made the map true to its word! After

having travelled for days and days in dense jungle, we suddenly left it behind, as if we had gone through a gigantic "door".

After a day on the road in Zaire

One minute we were immersed in the dark shadows of tall trees, and the next minute we were in the middle of an enormous expanse of open grassland, staring back at a "wall" of trees! It was here that the jungle ended so abruptly, like a straight line as far as the eye could see. We had entered the northern part of Virunga National Park, with our first view of some of the classic African animals that we looked forward to seeing later on the vast plains of East Africa. Throughout the day, as we travelled further south through the park, we spotted Cape Buffalo, Giraffe, and Gazelle. Far in the distance, we could see the Ruwenzori Mountains, as we headed that way. Later in the afternoon, we came to the small village of Atunukwe, where we were able to set up camp in a clearing on the edge of the village. And as usual, a group of children soon showed up to watch us making a campfire for cooking dinner later. Our cooking crew was able to buy a dozen eggs from one of the villagers to add to our dehydrated rations that night.

December 13 - 14, 1974
Atunukwe, Zaire - Beni, Zaire

"Tropical Rainstorm" or *"A Slippin and a Slidin"* We left camp early the next morning to begin the long, slow climb into the Ruwenzori Mountains of eastern Zaire, a beautiful region of steep hills covered in lush vegetation. Throughout the area, small villages clung to the steep hillsides, sometimes below us and at other times above the road. It was a very scenic drive, but as the day wore on, the skies darkened and eventually the inevitable tropical rain showers drenched the hills with cool water, as if to wake them from their drowsy afternoon nap! We were engulfed in the downpour just as we were trying to negotiate a rather tricky stretch of the mountain road. It wasn't long before the entire road turned into very sticky red mud.

Road through the jungle in Zaire

Stuart did some amazing driving while the old bus was constantly slipping and sliding all over the road.

We were doing exceptionally well, given the atrocious road conditions, until we came around a sharp curve and saw three African trucks hopelessly stuck in the middle of the road on a long downhill stretch. There was no way Stuart could get past the mess, so once again, when none of the locals seemed to be able to get it together, the SIAFU team sprang into action. Stuart and Dave were able to get everyone pushing together, and after considerable hard work and exasperation, we were able to get all three trucks out of the mud and moving again—even the truck with no battery or brakes! (Some of the old African trucks were held together with little more than duct tape, vines, and a prayer!)

Once we were underway again, we were invited to camp at a Methodist mission in the small town of Beni. As we set up camp that evening, the inevitable audience of local children showed up. The night was cool and damp, a welcome relief from the heat and humidity of the day. But the next morning, to our dismay, as Stuart and I checked the bus, we discovered a broken engine mount. Consulting the vehicle service manual, it was required to remove the entire engine in order to replace a broken engine mount. But what were we to do, stuck in the middle of Zaire?

So, with some considerable ingenuity and skill, we decided to use two jacks to raise one side of the engine just enough to allow us to access the broken mount. A few hours later, as Pink Floyd's album, "Dark Side of the Moon", played on my cassette tape player, we had installed a new engine mount, and both of us celebrated the accomplishment. At that moment, I felt like I had achieved the skill of a "bush mechanic", thanks to Stuart. It went without saying, that when John and I had signed up for this overland expedition, I had never anticipated having such an experience. But I had to admit that I liked working on the vehicles during the many mechanical breakdowns, rather than sitting on the sidelines with the rest of the group, waiting for so many hours and days! In the end, I knew I would definitely remember these most amazing repairs in the middle of nowhere as some of the greatest challenges of my time in Africa. Later, having completed the repair, we decided to spend another night camped at the mission. And our audience of local kids enjoyed another evening watching us go about our nightly routine of cooking dinner, cleaning up, and retiring for the night.

December 15, 1974
Beni, Zaire to Butembo, Zaire

"Dinner by Candlelight" The following morning we were back on the road, headed south to a large sugar plantation where they were able to finally repair the broken clutch pedal. With the repair complete, we continued our journey through the beautiful mountains, with the road weaving in and out of steep canyons, up and down high hills, and passing many small villages literally "clinging" to the steep slopes. At times, we would come to a high point on the road and were presented with a spectacular panorama of mountains stacked upon mountains, terraced fields overlapping each other, stretching as far as the eye could see. The scenes begged us to photograph them, and we all obliged. (I came to remember this region of Africa as the most beautiful place on earth!)

Late in the afternoon, the daily tropical rain showers arrived for their ritual cleansing of the countryside. And once again, the dirt road became a long "ribbon" of red mud, which Stuart managed to negotiate with considerable skill. However, it wasn't much further down the road before we encountered several African trucks stuck in an enormous, very nasty, mean mudhole. Navigating past the mud hole and the

trucks marooned in it, tested Stuart's prowess as an expert coach driver! Once we were successfully beyond the mud hole, we stopped to offer assistance to the trucks still stuck in the mud.

That evening we pulled into the small town of Butembo, by which time we were all soaking wet, cold and covered in red mud. That was when John came up with a splendid idea—he proposed that we stay the night at the one and only hotel in town and share a dinner there. For almost all of us, it sounded fantastic—although the Smiths and Seymour declined to join us, which we felt was just as well! John used his outstanding

PR skills to negotiate an amazingly low price with the hotel owner for dinner. The old French hotel was a classic place, but over the years, it had lost a lot of its luster and elegance. However, it still retained a few remnants of the grand old days to allow our imagination to fill in the details of its glorious past. That evening, we all sat down together to share a fine French dinner service in a small, cozy dining room, bathed in the soft light from a few candles—the electricity having been turned off earlier in the evening. For the next two hours, we enjoyed a delicious four-course dinner and a very pleasant, relaxed evening—a rare treat on our trip! (Thanks to John) Later, a few of us retired to our hotel room and relaxed in front of a roaring fireplace, listening to music from my cassette tape player. At that moment, we all agreed, it was a most pleasant and welcome break from life on the road!

December 16, 1974
Butembo, Zaire - Musienene, Zaire

"Just South of the Equator" or *"The other side of the World"* The following morning, we awoke to a beautiful day and continued our journey through the lush forest of the Ruwenzori Mountains, headed south towards Goma. We hadn't driven more than 10 or 15 miles before we came upon a small, rather inconspicuous (at least by American standards) sign that marked the location of an imaginary line dividing the Earth into two halves! It wasn't a particularly spectacular place, and easily passed over by most people, without noticing the sign. But it represented one of those clearly defined lines on every world map, that indicated what was north and south from where we stood! The "equator" was identified by this little wooden sign, upon which many overland groups had marked their progress and left messages for those who followed.

Crossing the equator in Zaire

So, we left our mark as well—"King Kong was here"!

Just then, Stuart and Dave celebrated the occasion by pulling up the sign and standing with it in front of King Kong for a series of photos. At that point, I pondered the question—"did the equator actually move?" As we replaced the sign, we now began our journey into the southern hemisphere, to the small village of Musienene. There we were able to set up camp in a clearing just outside the village and enjoyed an evening free of our usual "audience". Perhaps the children hadn't noticed us, or maybe their parents respected our privacy. Either way, it was appreciated.

December 17–19, 1974
Musienene, Zaire - Kishumburi, Zaire

"The Most Pleasant Breakdown" As we continued our trip south, higher and higher into the Ruwenzori Mountains, we passed beautiful vistas of hazy hills and valleys.

Kivu Volcanoes in the Ruwenzori Mountains, Zaire

The unpaved road wound its way through grassy fields and tall forests—an incredible variety of lovely scenery awaited us around every turn, as we ventured further south into the "bottom half" of the world! The experience of the Ruwenzori region kept growing upon my memory as a beautiful, tranquil, peaceful world of its own—a veritable kingdom in Africa, hidden from the rest of the world.

Villages in the Ruwenzori Mountains

Our time seemed to pass so pleasantly and at such a timeless pace, that when the front wheel of the bus suddenly fell off, we all just took it in the calmness of the moment that had been instilled within us so subtly by the landscape around us.

King Kong with a broken front axle

As the old bus came to an abrupt halt in the middle of the road, there was little agitation or anger at our incredible bad luck. There was no confusion about what to do—we turned our back on the "ghost of mechanical failures" and calmly set about establishing camp in a lush field beside the road, next to the crippled body of King Kong. As we pitched our tents in the deep green grass, we seemed to be in the middle of a plush carpet, overlooking the hills above us and a small village below.

Camped in the Ruwenzori Mountains, Zaire

Looking to the west, we could see a collection of old yellow brick buildings upon the crest of a high grassy knoll. It had the appearance of an old English farm, with cows grazing in the pasture below—a most beautiful setting. A John Constable painting of it would have been titled "A Pastoral Scene"—so quiet, peaceful, and in perfect harmony with the landscape!

Belgian dairy farm in the Ruwenzori Mountains

Throughout the coming days, the sunlight painted many different colors on the farm and fields, more than any artist could have attempted. Night was the only rival of the beauty of the day, when millions of stars were spread from hill to hill across the full expanse of the black night sky. It was also a time when a cold chill crept upon the land, to lay in rest until the sun rose the next morning to chase it away. During the afternoons, the inevitable mountain showers announced the approach of evening with the soft pattering of rain drops on our tent roof. The landscape flourished with the combination of chilly night air and daily rain showers. It gave us the impression of being anywhere in the world but just south of the equator. The feeling was very refreshing and invigorating, like stepping into an icy mountain stream. The ever-changing clouds hanging over the mountains added a distinctive element to create a very peaceful, serene landscape. One afternoon, a few of us were invited by the Belgian owner of the dairy farm on the hill above our camp to sample his cream, butter, and cheese. We soon purchased a couple liters of cream, a kilo of butter, and a large block of white cheddar cheese, which certainly "enhanced" our dinner that night. Krem spent a couple of hours struggling to get a good fire going, with the only wood available being pretty wet from the daily tropical rain showers. His valiant efforts were watched by a small group of local kids who were fascinated by the whole process. In the end, his work paid off and we all enjoyed a tasty dinner. Sitting around the campfire, there was general agreement among the group that this was the "most pleasant breakdown".

In the meantime, Stuart and Dave had been fortunate to find a local Belgian mechanic who was able to weld the stub axel and get the bus running again.

December 19, 1974
Kishumburi, Zaire – Nyiragongo Volcano, Zaire

"*The Long Hard Climb*" We were sad to leave our beautiful hillside camp in the heart of the Ruwenzori, but also happy to be back on the road again. Gradually we left the mountains and came upon a unique geological phenomenon known as the "Kabasha Escarpment" which divided Lake

Edward in the north from Lake Kivu in the south, along the Albertine Rift. As we descended the rim of the escarpment, we had a magnificent panorama of Lake Edward and the Albertine Rift Valley. Soon we were entering the southern half of Virunga National Park far below. Slowly, we descended on a narrow, twisting dirt road, over 4000 feet down to the valley floor. As we made our way through the expanse of the valley, we saw large herds of Antelope, Giraffe, Elephant, and Cape Buffalo.

Coming out of the jungle in Zaire

That evening, we found a lovely campsite on the short grass plain beside a small river, near where a group of Hippos were gathered. As we went about setting up camp, we realized we were within sight of several majestic volcanoes in the Kivu region to the south.

Virunga National Park, Zaire

It was a perfect campsite, and I took the opportunity to take a quick dip in the river, among a grove of palm trees and flowering bushes, just before dusk. Afterwards, it was a most refreshing feeling as I sat down to dinner in front of a roaring campfire. Little did I realize at the time, while I had been splashing around in the river, I had not been alone— the Hippos had been just upstream and around the bend!

The next morning, we awoke to a spectacular view of the volcanoes, shrouded in clouds rising high above the grassy plains, and bathed in the soft orange glow of the rising sun. Among the chain of mountains was an active volcano named Nyiragongo, rising above 11,000 feet.

Mt Nyiragongo, Ruwenzori Mountains, Zaire

It wasn't long before Stuart began organizing a small group of us to climb the summit of the volcano. Later that afternoon, we met up with our local guide at the foot of the mountain for the 4-hour climb to the summit. He was a large black man named "Big John", with a very tough, weathered face, large muscular features, and a pair of absolutely incredible feet that looked tougher than my French mountain climbing boots. The soles of his feet must have been at least an inch thick, covered in callouses from what must have been the result of hundreds of miles of climbing in the mountains. But what impressed me most was his agility and ease in hiking "barefoot" up the steep, rocky trail to the summit! Any ordinary person would have had nothing but bloody, shredded stumps for feet after such a climb—but not Big John! His bare feet survived the sharp lava rock and steep slopes with nothing more than a few scratches—it had to be a story for "Ripley's Believe It or Not".

The first couple of miles on the trail were relatively flat, winding through forest in the low foothills, before beginning the slow, steep climb up the lava slope. As our group slowly stumbled up the steep, rocky trail, we started to experience the effects of the high altitude above 8,000 feet. The last few hundred yards were almost straight up, and I found it to be very strenuous, not having tackled such a high mountain since my climbing days in Montana several years before. But finally, after 3 hours of hard labor, I reached the climber's hut at 11,000 feet elevation, where we would spend the night. Sometime later, the rest of our group arrived at the hut. By this time the sun had set, and it was very cold and windy—not one's vision of equatorial Africa, rather more like regions several thousand miles to the north. It was nature's way of playing a joke on our senses! Then we gathered outside in the darkness, and our guide led us on a short climb over massive piles of lava rock, up to the rim of the crater.

When we reached the edge, we were rewarded with a spectacular view of a large lake of bubbling red-hot lava and fountains of fire! (While we had been camped on the grassy plains of Virunga National Park the night before, we had seen the red glow from the lava atop the volcano more than 60 miles to the south.) We sat on the rim in the midst of the lava rock for almost two hours, while a raw, icy wind whirled around us, before we all gave in to our desire for hot food and a warm sleeping bag. The way back down the steep rocky slope was a bit scary as we slid down the sharp lava rock on our backsides! The night remained very windy and quite cold, well below freezing, which yielded sleep at a premium. Early the next morning, the sunrise was incredible, with the mountains to the east in Rwanda silhouetted against a gorgeous soft orange glow in the sky. As we made our way down the mountain, we had gained a great respect for its enormous size and immense place in the world. As well, I felt a great sense of satisfaction and achievement at having met the mountain on some of its own terms—but to claim that I had "conquered" it would not only have been an exaggeration of my skill, but a gross injustice to the mountain as well, whose elements were formidable. It was more appropriate to say that Nyiragongo allowed me the chance to scale its heights and witness its primitive beauty!

December 20, 1974
Goma, Zaire – Gisenyi, Rwanda

"The Gardens of the Ruwenzori" Once we were back down from the mountain, and rejuvenated with greater strength, we headed to the beautiful colonial town of Goma, situated on the shore of Lake Kivu. Along the road to Goma, we came upon a roadside farmers market where they had an amazing display of local fruits and vegetables, all of which were of enormous size. Our eyes could hardly believe the sight of huge, fresh crisp carrots, cabbage, avocado, cauliflower, onions, artichokes, bananas and much more! A wild buying spree ensued, as our cooking crew attempted to buy everything in sight. After stuffing the storage cabinets in the back of the bus full of all manner of fresh produce, we found our total expenditure had been the local equivalent of $4.00—a fantastic bargain!

As we entered the old Belgian town, we rendezvoused with John, who had been on another of his sojourns, following our breakdown in the Ruwenzori Mountains. We spent a couple of hours in Goma, visiting the French patisserie for delicious delights and a Belgian coffee house as well. So, it was a very pleasant visit to Goma, a modern town and home to many Europeans. The beauty and primary appeal of the town was its location in a spectacular landscape of mountains surrounding Lake Kivu, as well as the lovely, moderate year-round climate of the equatorial region. Later in the afternoon, we left Goma and headed east to the small town of Gisenyi, just over the border in Rwanda. After the usual customs and immigration delays, inherent in every border crossing, we stopped to have lunch along the eastern shore of Lake Kivu. It was a very relaxing moment, devoid of any mechanical problems.

As we continued our route toward Kigali, the capitol of Rwanda, we discovered it to be a beautiful country, more highly developed than Zaire. The western region was quite mountainous, with steep slopes cultivated in a series of lovely terraced fields all the way to the top. The high fertility of the region was the result of volcanic activity over thousands of years, making Rwanda one of the most fertile regions in Africa. Not only was it one of the smallest countries in Africa, it also had a high population density.

With evening approaching, our cooking crew prepared an amazing BBQ alongside the road, using the abundance of fresh produce from the farmers market north of Goma, along with a small supply of fresh meat we had picked up in Goma. The meal was a most welcome change from the incredibly boring menu of dehydrated foods.

Chapter six

December 21-23, 1974
Gisenyi, Rwanda - Kigali, Rwanda

"Hit the road Jack " A late night drive, following the evening BBQ, put us within 10 miles of Kigali the next morning, so we hurried toward the city in the hope of finding a lot of mail awaiting us. There was also the chance, unlikely, but worth a try, of securing visas for travel through Uganda that would enable us to arrive in Nairobi before Christmas, just a few days away. Kigali was located on the summit of a high escarpment above a large river, and the only access was by of a very steep, winding road. Stuart did his best to coax every bit of speed from Kong, being forced to negotiate the steep grade in first gear, even so, we barely made it!

Then we rushed to the Post Office, only to discover to our great dismay and disappointment, there was NO mail awaiting our delayed arrival. Apparently, SIAFU headquarters in London had forwarded it on to Nairobi for the group ahead of us in the truck. We were not happy, to say the least! And on top of that, we learned the Ugandan ambassador was out of the office for the weekend and it was closed. So, there was no chance for visas until Monday morning. As we all tried our best to deal with the disappointments, John and I decided to do a tour of Kigali. After an hour or so, a Time magazine, a copy of the International Herald

Tribune newspaper, and a couple cups of tea, we realized we had seen Kigali!

The capitol was not a bustling metropolis by any means, and in fact, the Presidential Palace was so innocuous that we hardly noticed it. The Post Office was twice as large and a lot more elegant. After having taken in all the sights of the city, we drove back down the hill to set up camp for the weekend, in anticipation of being able to check back with the Ugandan embassy on Monday. We were lucky to discover another abandoned gravel quarry beside a small river, and well hidden from the main road. The surrounding countryside was a beautiful river valley, with lovely hills and terraced fields that reminded me of the Mosel Valley wine region of Germany. Our short stay was very pleasant and comfortable, with only a small "audience" occasionally.

On Sunday afternoon, we got up enough energy to do a thorough "bang up" job of cleaning the old bus inside and out. As so often happens with this kind of project, one thing led to another, and when we were

finished, the entire bus was spotless. The storage cabinets had also been taken out and refitted, so that by the end of the day, we almost had a brand-new bus! Though in reality, we still had all the mechanical bugs with us, just in a new box now, so to speak—ready to hit the open road again.

December 24, 1974
Kigali, Rwanda – Mobeye, Tanzania

"Christmas Eve—African Mass" Monday morning, after breaking camp, we drove back up the hill to Kigali, anxious to find out if we could get visas to travel to Nairobi through Uganda. It would have meant being able to arrive in Nairobi before Christmas, something we had all secretly banked on. But, as it turned out, we were denied Ugandan visas, a real let down for all of us. Before leaving Kigali, I managed to send a short telegram from the main Post Office to my parents in Florida, wishing them Merry Christmas and Happy New Year! As I walked out of the Post Office, I knew I would have no way of knowing if they received it or not, for I would be out of contact for the next 10 days as we continued our

105

journey through Tanzania to Nairobi. We bid farewell to Rwanda and hello to Tanzania at a place called Rusumo Falls, near the most distant headwaters of the Nile River.

Along the way from Kigali, we passed a couple of Chinese trucks and their workers constructing roads and building bridges, as part of an economic aid program for Rwanda. Before crossing the border, we put on our finest "duds", in an attempt to look like honest to goodness paying tourists, not some common "overlanders". For the past few months on the road, we had been wearing just grubby jeans or shorts and dirty T-shirts. As we approached the border station, I had to wonder if the immigration officials really believed we travelled in such nice clean clothes, through hundreds of miles of dust, mud, and rain—but the effort to look "presentable" worked well and we proceeded into Tanzania with a minimum of delay. By this time, all of us were feeling very nostalgic, remembering how we had always celebrated Christmas with our families. Before now, there had been little time to anticipate Christmas, but as we rumbled across the plains of East Africa, the realization of this day being Christmas Eve suddenly and unexpectedly crept upon us. As evening approached, we made a vain attempt at singing Christmas carols, but our hearts and spirits weren't really up to it.

Meanwhile, Stuart and Dave were looking for a nice place to set up camp, somewhere alongside the road. The wide expanse of the open grassland looked very inviting, but as we pulled off to the side of the road and stepped out of the bus, we were immediately attacked by swarms of tsetse flies! It was all we could do to beat a hasty retreat to the bus and get back on the road. We had no choice but to press on as darkness fell. Further down the road, we began seeing a lot of local people walking along the edge of the road, toward a village ahead. As we came into the village, we could see everyone was making their way to a chapel next to a German mission and seminary.

When we stopped at the mission, we were warmly welcomed to camp for the night. Marion and Ginny prepared a delicious supper that evening, and afterwards, some of us decided to make our way to the chapel for the midnight Mass. The chapel was very crowded, but as we approached the door, a priest spotted us and insisted that we join a group of nuns seated inside. He proceeded to usher us into the middle of the chapel, where the nuns graciously invited us to sit with them. The celebration of Christmas Mass was much the same as elsewhere in the world, except for two unique differences. The entire Mass was conducted in the local Swahili language and accompanied by native African music. The sound of the voices and the traditional rhythm of the drums gave the ceremony a wonderful feeling of spontaneity, joy, happiness and even laughter at times. It was a light and joyous sound that the whole congregation felt move through their bodies in rhythm with the music. As I listened to the Mass, I felt it made Christmas a joyous time and a happy birthday, as it was meant to be! (That night remained etched in my memory forever!)

December 25-26, 1974
Mobeye, Tanzania - Mwanza, Tanzania

"Christmas in Africa" On Christmas morning, we got our first glimpse of Lake Victoria as we boarded a ferry that would take us across the southern arm of the lake to the town of Mwanza. While on the ferry, John struck up a conversation with some young Indian folks who gave him the names of a few places they recommended for food and accommodations in the town. Upon arriving in Mwanza, we were all looking forward to having a proper Christmas dinner together that evening. But, as expected, the Smiths and Seymour were too cheap to stay in a hotel or eat out. We all felt it was just as well, since we couldn't stand having them around anyway. So, four of us (John, Ginny, Marion, and myself) checked into a nice hotel room for about $1.50 per night, which included a warm shower to boot.

Later that evening, after having "freshened up", we all sat down to a lovely dinner in the hotel restaurant with the rest of our group and wished everyone around the table a Merry Christmas! Afterwards, the four of us walked over to the New Mwanza Hotel and shared a small bottle of brandy, as we exchanged some small gifts. It was a very special moment for each of us that night as we thought of our families several thousands of miles away. We spent the rest of the evening listening and dancing to a band from Zaire, with their signature heavy "Zaire beat".

Then we returned to our hotel room, where we encountered loud music coming from an Indian band, featuring several black musicians and singers, the sound of which was being blasted from a large loudspeaker just 50 feet from our door! The band finally called it a night at 2:00 am, allowing us a few hours sleep. The next morning was spent in town, buying a few supplies, touring the public market, and having lunch at the New Mwanza Hotel, overlooking Lake Victoria. Then, late in the afternoon, we were back on the road and headed northeast toward Serengeti National Park, a place we were all eagerly looking forward to visiting.

That night, we made camp just south of the park, on the shore of Lake Victoria. It looked like a beautiful location, but the lake was infested with Bilharzia and home to billions of mosquitoes! So, there was no chance of bathing in the lake, or even approaching the water, unfortunately. After dinner, as we were getting ready to retire for the night, John discovered that all but one of the jerry cans of water had been lost, which suddenly put us in a difficult bind—having to "ration" water, as we had done so many times in the Sahara. Apparently, the cans had fallen off the side of the bus somewhere along the road from Mwanza.

December 27-28, 1974
Mwanza, Tanzania – Serengeti National Park – Ngorongoro Crater

"Plains of East Africa—On Safari" We awoke early the next morning, in great anticipation of finally visiting the world's most famous game park in East Africa. But earlier, while we were on the ferry to Mwanza, we had heard from another overland group that the road into the western corridor of the park was in very bad condition as a result of recent rains. Evidently, it had taken them more than 4 hours to travel less than 12 miles. So, we prepared for the worst by connecting the front draft shaft again. Now ready to do battle with the muddy road, we arrived at the park gate, only to find it closed due the recent heavy rains! The only alternate route was further north to a road that bypassed the western portion of the park.

Entering Serengeti National Park, Tanzania

Late that afternoon, we were able to enter the northern gate to the park and set up camp among some huge rocks, known as a "kopje", not far from Seronera Lodge.

I had just finished pitching our tent, when out of the darkness appeared John and Rabia, the couple from Canada who had decided to leave the expedition in Kano and fly on to Nairobi. They had been away from our group for almost three months, so it was really good to see them again and to share our stories. They were on their way to Dar Es Salam, having just come from Nairobi. They joined us for dinner around the campfire that evening, before returning to Seronera Lodge for the night. We enjoyed a spectacular sunset on the plains of East Africa that evening, and as we climbed into our tents, the sounds of elephants, lions, and hyenas echoed in the darkness. It was just like I had always imagined it would be, camped on the plains of East Africa—a dream had been fulfilled!

We arose very early the next morning, even before the sunrise, in order to get an early start for our first day's drive through the park.

The sunrise was absolutely beyond description, hopefully expressed in my photos. At that moment, I had to marvel when I looked back on how many sunrises, I had seen on the trip so far, in Africa more than anywhere else. The early mornings seemed to really agree with me, now more than ever. As we drove through the western corridor of the park, the scene was straight out of a National Geographic documentary film. There was an abundance of large game, especially Giraffe, very graceful when running at full gallop across the plains. Our cameras clicked away at a phenomenal rate, from all sides of the bus. It was almost like a big game hunting safari of bygone days, with all the talk of "shots" of various animals. Even the stoic Barton Smith was moved to shoot a couple of photos, though as we all knew by now, New Zealand had more and better animals, among the best of everything else!

The experience of being in Serengeti slowly formed a deep impression on me, that of being only a brief visitor in the natural environment of animals I had only known in a zoo. Now, as we sat in the bus taking photos, it seemed that we were the ones in a "cage", moving through the heart of Africa where the animals could watch us from a safe distance! It struck me at that moment, about how a zoo would be a different place for me now. Instead of seeing the animals in cages, I would remember them as they ran free across the plains of East Africa.

As the lunch hour approached, we decided to stop at Seronera Lodge, and as we made our way to the bar, it became readily apparent that most of us were painfully "out of our element". All around us were the "beautiful people", Jetsetters, and wealthy international snobs and bores. It was obvious by the look of our road worn clothes that we were travelling overland, and stares came from every corner of the room! (For us, we felt it was a "compliment", rather than an insult. In that atmosphere, we enjoyed the wonderful luncheon buffet—a special treat to celebrate our arrival in Serengeti.

After a delicious and relaxing lunch, we boarded our old bus and headed east, out of the park toward our next destination, Ngorongoro Crater National Park. Along the way, we were fortunate to see a Cheetah, asleep in the tall grass, just a few yards from the road. And a short time later, we came upon a pack of African Wild Dogs—not often seen during daylight hours. Just then, we felt some weird vibrations and heard strange noises.

Upon investigation, Stuart and I found it coming from the right front wheel—the same one that had broken in the Ruwenzori Mountains. As we looked closer, we discovered the problem, a bad wheel bearing, which caused the whole wheel assembly to shimmy and shake even worse than usual. In addition, the engine in the old bus had great difficulty negotiating the steep road to the top of Ngorongoro Crater—Kong's power had slowly "aged" since our repairs in the Sahara Desert three months earlier. There was no alternative but to press on up the steep road to the rim of the ancient volcanic crater. After a painfully long, slow climb in first gear up the steep slope of the crater, we finally arrived at the National Park campsite, a beautiful clearing on the very edge of the crater rim. Some of us took advantage of the hot shower facilities before dinner. That evening, as the sun set behind us, we had a spectacular view of the entire crater bathed in the soft glow of a full moon. Then a cold, clear night crept upon the crater to embrace us until morning

December 29–30, 1974
Ngorongoro Crater - Arusha, Tanzania

"A World of its Own" An incredible sunrise greeted us early the next morning, a great beginning to a day we were all anticipating with excitement—a wildlife tour of the crater!

Sunrise - Ngorongoro Crater, Tanzania

Unfortunately, we weren't able to book a tour until late afternoon, so we spent the morning in the lodge overlooking the crater through a massive wall of glass. The old lodge was a classic national park design of natural wood and stone architecture, which added a beautiful element to the lovely view and our experience in the lodge. As we sat in front of the huge windows, sipping our coffee, we watched puffy white clouds slowly floating over the crater, playing "hide-n-seek" with the sun.

Ngorongoro Crater National Park, Tanzania

Meanwhile, we wrote letters, postcards, and in my case, additions to my journal.

At one point, I looked up from writing and saw a large group of Marabou Storks "strolling" back and forth in front of the lodge, as if they were "caretakers" in charge of the lodge. They were tall, stately birds and quite formal in their appearance and manners. Occasionally, when a group of them were strolling together, they looked like old English statesmen, just having come from Parliament, discussing some serious world problem, with their hands clasped behind their back and staring intensely at the ground in front of them. In reality, the storks were very busy looking for a meal of bugs and worms in the grass.

We also had the good fortune to be spectators for an amazing aerial show, put on by the local Eagles and the stately storks. As we watched from the lodge, they would soar high over the rim of the crater, riding on the strong updrafts of warm air rising from below, for what seemed like hours. There were times when they appeared almost motionless—hanging in mid-air as the wind rushed past their enormous outstretched wings. At that moment, my only thought was—"Ah, to be a bird"! And as for the giant storks, it was an incredible sight to see them come in for a landing. They glided down slowly, with their enormous black wings, spread out over 6 feet, and long legs hanging beneath them, at the ready for touchdown. I imagined it to be very much like watching a 747 land at O'Hare airport. I was pretty sure it must have taken as much skill to land as well. And so, the morning passed quietly, as we were entranced by the aerial display and antics of the resident avian population.

Later, that afternoon, we got our chance to do a wildlife tour down in the crater—a very unique place and like no other in the world. At the lodge we met up with our guides/drivers and piled into the waiting Land Rovers for the trip down to the floor of the crater. Over the next half hour, we endured a "rough and tumble" journey down 3000 feet to the bottom of the crater, along a very steep, narrow road that was quite rough in places. As we arrived at the crater floor, we had a spectacular panorama of the entire caldera. Its immense size was overwhelming, almost like being on another planet. We were surrounded on all sides by high mountains, as if in the center of a gigantic valley.

Once we were on the crater floor, we drove to the edge of a massive shallow lake, covered with thousands of brilliant pink flamingoes, all standing knee deep in the bright blue water.

Flamingoes - Ngorongoro Crater

I noticed the intermittent sunshine slowly turned the color of the birds from light red to subtle pink as clouds passed over the lake, while the water transformed from blue to light grey, in unison with the change in the color of the flamingoes. Occasionally, something would "spook" the birds and they would all react at the same time and move in the same direction. It was like watching a military regiment doing close order drill—a fascinating natural behavior. Over the course of the afternoon, an incredible array of wildlife passed before our eyes, and at such close quarters, we could almost reach out and touch them!

Lions in Ngorongoro Crater

There were lions, elephants, rhino, hippos, cape buffalo, and wildebeest—all poised for our cameras, as the Land Rovers slowly made their way among them.

It soon became clear that Ngorongoro Crater was a world of its own, where we were merely momentary visitors. As we began to make our way back up to the lodge, we came upon a small grove of trees beside the lake. By this time in the late afternoon, the sunlight had become a soft golden color that "accented" the subtle contrast of the pale shades of green and gold from the leaves and tree bark. At the same time, rays of sunlight pierced the canopy like spears of gold! And standing in the middle of the grove's soft beauty was an old elephant, quietly grazing in the thick, dark green carpet of lush grass. With the spectacular background of the high crater wall, it was a classic photo in every sense of the word, and a perfect conclusion to our tour of the crater!

The ride back to the lodge up the steep embankment was chilly, and yet invigorating at the same time. We were prepared to leave the national park as soon as we returned to the lodge, since technically we had stayed beyond the time that we had been allowed upon entering the park the day before. But of even more concern, the park gate would close soon! We were only a few miles down the road, when the ghost of mechanical failures arose from his slumber—the motor sputtered to a halt and died. Our beautiful day quickly faded into a dreary state of depression. Stuart, Dave and I looked at each other and our eyes told the same story—"What was it now?" Our first response was to check the fuel line, the cause of so many problems in the past. But what we found was an empty fuel tank! Apparently, Kong had used an unbelievable amount of fuel during the past several days.

So, while Stuart and Dave hitched a ride back to the lodge to get some diesel fuel, the rest of us sat in the cold, dark bus, conjuring up vivid images of our favorite holiday foods, which tantalized everyone's taste buds. I had to admit, there were some very tasty descriptions, but none of them were filling. After an hour or so, Stuart and Dave returned with a jerry can of diesel fuel and we were on our way again—although everyone was tired and hungry by that time. As we approached the park gate in the evening darkness, the park ranger was very nice and understanding, letting us exit without a fine—something Stuart had been very worried about. Once outside the national park boundary, we found a small clearing alongside the road and set up camp for the night.

The following day, we drove to Lake Manyara and stopped at a spectacular vista point on top of the escarpment overlooking the lake. The panoramic view of the lake, valley, and plains in the distance on the eastern horizon was incredible! Many of us took photos beside our "beloved" King Kong before we left the lake. As we descended further down the road, we came upon a lovely mountain stream, just begging us to jump in! Naturally, we couldn't refuse the invitation. But just as we finished splashing cold water over ourselves, we were confronted by an angry national park ranger who was very irate that some of us had bathed in the "national park side" of the stream—apparently the other side was legal, despite the water being common to both sides! He proceeded to threaten us with a fine of 50 schillings each, and said he was going to escort us to the local police station. About this time came the inevitable comment from Bartie—"I could have told you this would happen"! It did nothing to make the situation any more acceptable. As it turned out, while we were being led toward the police station, the park ranger suddenly pulled over and waved us on—for what reason we didn't know and didn't bother to ask! (We never had the chance to tell our side of the story to the authorities, but neither did we care to.)

Then came the moment we had all been looking forward to for so many months, a modern paved high-way and a road sign, "Nairobi 575 km"! From this point it was a short hop to the town of Arusha, located in the foothills of Mt Kilimanjaro. The town had many "delights" we had eagerly been anticipating—ice cream, hamburgers, and cold beer! We were also able to find the latest Time magazine and International Herald Tribune, which helped put us back in the present day. I also purchased a small bottle of brandy for New Year's Eve, just two days away. Suddenly, Dave discovered he had lost his money pouch and all his money—it was a devastating moment for him.

As he looked back, he figured he must have accidentally left it at the Ngorongoro Lodge when he and Stuart had returned to purchase the diesel fuel. So, he and Stuart made a trip to the local police station to file a report, but there was little chance of the money being recovered. Meanwhile, the rest of us took the opportunity to browse through the arts and crafts shops in the center of town. In one shop, I found some local Makonde wood carvings—very unique for their abstract depiction of animals and people. In many aspects, they resembled modern sculpture, yet with a very traditional style—simply beautiful! Then, as we were about to leave Arusha, John scored a quick deal for some dope, trading one of my old, greasy t-shirts for a small "lid".

Later, as the evening fell upon us, we stopped alongside the highway at the base of Mt Meru. But what we discovered on the only level ground was an abundance of sand, gravel and some vicious thorns! Despite the rough ground and nasty thorns, the night was stupendous—clear, cool and quiet, like so many nights we had spent in the Sahara! Warm and lovely memories of nights in the desert filled my head as I lay on the sand, bathed in the brilliant light of a full moon and gently caressed by a cool night breeze. As I fell asleep, I looked forward to celebrating New Year's Eve and the beginning of another year—1975!

December 31, 1974
Arusha, Tanzania - Amboseli National Park, Kenya

"It's Really Kenya" or *"It's New Year's Eve"* By the next morning, almost everyone had suffered some sort of injury from the nasty thorns—including one in my knuckle that was destined to become infected! We were up early, just as the sun rose above the summit of Mt Meru. As we quickly broke camp, there was a renewed spirit among the group, as we all realized our elusive goal of reaching Nairobi was at last within our grasp! It was less than 20 miles to the border with Kenya, and as we crossed it, we felt "thousands" of miles closer to realizing that goal. The border crossing formalities were minimal, which surprised us, since it was the only border station open at the time. We were told that a border dispute had developed recently when Kenya closed the border to halt the spread of a cholera epidemic from Kisumu, Tanzania. That resulted in a retaliation by Tanzania and placed severe weight restrictions on KENATCO trucks (National Transportation Company of Kenya travelling into Tanzania. Soon, a full closure of the border followed, except for the border crossing on the main highway from Nairobi. It remained open to enable large numbers of foreign tourists to pass back and forth between the two countries. (Money does have a loud voice!

After crossing into Kenya, Stuart stopped to call a short meeting of the group and discuss plans for the next two days. The choices were (1 drive straight to Nairobi that same day or (2 spend New Year's Eve in Amboseli National Park before going on to Nairobi the next day. Seeing that we had already spent almost four months on the road, what difference would two days make now. And besides, Amboseli was a place we all wanted to experience. It was a unanimous decision—Amboseli. As we drove toward the national park, we were passing through the land of the Maasai, a region of harsh plains inhabited by distinctive people— tall, slender and stately, dressed very much in the traditional style of their ancestors. They lived entirely off the land and their cattle, as they had done for generations. Their large herds of cattle sustained them with a concoction of milk, blood, and urine—rarely did they slaughter a cow, and then only for a very special occasion. The Maasai warriors had very fine facial features, long braided black hair caked with red mud, lots of jewelry in their ears and around their neck, and often seen carrying a tall, pointed spear of metal and wood.

Young Maasai warrior - Kenya

They were truly interesting people who gave us the strong impression of being very aware of the 20th century, but not interested in what it might hold for them. They respected our western culture but were not about to compromise their own—something I came to respect very much.

Late in the afternoon, as we approached the national park lodge, the skies suddenly turned from clear blue to grey and eventually an ominous black. Soon, a powerful storm of intense proportions was about to descend upon us! Sure enough, it arrived with a vengeance—all the fury of a full-blown thunderstorm. Heavy rain pelted the roof of the bus and a strong wind whistled past the windows, almost daring us to come out and face it. The once dry, dusty plains were quickly transformed into enormous shallow lakes that foretold of deep mud to come later. It wasn't long before Kong was bouncing along through the shallow water, immersed in rain and mud. As quickly as the storm had arrived, it moved on, and the water was sucked up by the earth in a matter of minutes, testifying to its parched condition a few minutes before. Soon the air became calm again and a faint glimmer of sunshine peeked out through the broken clouds. We had been formally introduced to the season of the "short rains" in East Africa.

After a brief stop at the lodge to check in, several of us made reservations for dinner that evening. Then we made our way to the national park campground, a very nice spot among a grove of trees, about a half mile from the lodge. Although it was a familiar routine of unloading the gear and pitching tents, it felt special because it was New Year's Eve! Having established camp, most of us dressed in our finest clothes, which wasn't saying much, and climbed aboard King Kong for the short ride to the lodge, since it wasn't permitted to walk outside the campground because of the danger presented by wild animals. (Also, it could have resulted in a fine of 1,000 schillings. Upon arriving at the lodge, our special group of four (John, Ginny, Marion, and I were shown to our own table. Over the next two hours, we enjoyed an amazing evening, stuffing ourselves with all the delights of the incredible New Year's Eve feast—a seven course meal fit for a king! After having taken second and third helpings of everything, especially the scrumptious brandy bread pudding, we "waddled" into the lounge for coffee and light conversation.

As the witching hour of midnight approached, I sensed something was missing, namely music. There was not a sound to be heard anywhere, save for the soft clinking of dishes being washed in the kitchen and the quiet chatter among a few lodge residents. In order to remedy the awful situation, I grabbed my cassette tape player from the bus, as well as the bottle of brandy we had saved for the occasion. We listened intently to the music of Pink Floyd's album "Dark Side of the Moon", as we had done so many times before during the numerous mechanical breakdowns we had encountered on our four-month journey. Just like Stuart and Dave, I had developed a deep bond with the album, recalling all the difficult and challenging times, yet some of the most memorable.

As Pink Floyd continued to play into the night, it became closer and closer to midnight, when all of a sudden, the year became 1975! At that moment, we all gathered together, opened the brandy, toasted the New Year and sang Auld Lang Syne! It was quite a feat for us to still be awake at such a late hour, as we had made a habit of going to sleep with the sunset and getting up with the sunrise. But this evening was special—it was now 1975, and to keep the revelry going, we persuaded Scottish John to sing his favorite beer drinking song, a very traditional one from old Scotland called "The Wee Cock Sparrow". It was about a young boy who shot at a "wee" cock sparrow sitting on a fence and ended up hitting a man pushing a wheelbarrow with one of his arrows. It was a simple song, but what made it so hilarious was the pronunciation of the words by Scottish John. "Sparrow", "barrow" and "arrow" came out sounding like "sparra", "barra", and "arra", all in a high-pitched voice! He gave an amazing performance, and we all had a really good laugh with him, before we headed back to camp. For being New Year's Eve, our celebration was a quiet but most enjoyable one!

January 1, 1975
Amboseli National Park, Kenya

Mt Kilimanjaro - Amboseli National Park, Kenya

"In the Shadow of Mt Kilimanjaro" Most of us, at least those who had celebrated at the lodge, awoke rather late to the shouting of Mrs. Smith trying to cope with a band of thieving monkeys who resided in the trees above our camp. The little devils would snitch food off the plates on our table, right from under our noses! As I poked my head out of the tent, I saw Mrs. Smith frantically rushing around camp, trying desperately to keep the monkeys from ripping off our food, and at the same time, trying to get breakfast together. It was most disturbing, and the commotion made it impossible to sleep any later in the morning. So, we arose from our slumber and prepared to join Mrs. Smith and the monkeys. No sooner had I cut a slice of bread to make toast than a little, brown furry hand suddenly popped up and snatched it! The little hairy rascals were literally everywhere—one had to keep everything that was edible under virtual lock and key. But after a while, with breakfast over, I had to admit we soon enjoyed feeding the monkeys and watching them swing from limb to limb in the trees above us. In fact, I began to find them

more interesting, friendlier, and possessing of better table manners than a few members of our group! Later in the morning, Stuart decided we should take a short drive through the park to view the wildlife, and then perhaps to stop by the lodge for lunch.

As we drove the old bus out into the bush, following well-worn tracks of other vehicles, we all shared a feeling that our eternal nemesis, the ghost of mechanical failures, was constantly riding on our shoulders. And I was sure, as was Stuart, the demon was just waiting for the most opportune time to do his devilish deeds once again. Considering that our battery was dead, and we had been "push starting" the old bus for several days, the whole idea of driving anywhere had become paranoiac for all of us. I knew Stuart was feeling very apprehensive about doing a tour of the park, yet at the same time, excited to see the wildlife in the park, as we all were. With all this on our minds, we went bouncing over the vast plains, sliding across the mud left over from recent rain, until the inevitable happened—bound to sooner or later! As Stuart tried to skirt around a particularly nasty stretch of mud, the old beast slid off the main track and became stuck. Our predicament was made even worse by the fact we had busted the bolts on the front drive shaft several days before and had to remove it.

So, here we sat, stuck in the mud without 4-wheel drive. Perhaps we were destined to remain in the mud until someone happened by to help us, which might have been a very long time, especially with no other vehicles in sight! The option of walking back to the lodge was out of the question, considering the distance and the presence of wild animals, especially lions. So, we went about making our best efforts to get Kong out of the mud by chucking tree bark and limbs under the rear wheels, while we all pushed with all our strength. Despite our hard labor, the old beast just continued to "wallow" in the mud like a drunken Hippo on a Saturday night! It was at that point, Stuart decided to give it one more go and called upon all the muscle Kong had left to drag himself out of the mess. With a mighty roar from the exhaust, and a slick spin of the wheels, the huge bulk of the machine "lurched" backward on to a patch of dry land.

Suddenly, we were free at last, much to our astonishment and great relief! We made a hasty retreat to the lodge, and a welcome return to safety. To celebrate our victory over the mud, John treated me to a fabulous lunch buffet in the lodge, and once again, we stuffed ourselves. Following the delicious lunch, we took our coffee in the lounge next door for a relaxing bit of reading, writing, and conversation. And so, the afternoon passed quietly. Later that evening, the four of us once again shared dinner in the lodge, where we sampled more fantastic culinary delights, in preference to the horrid "bachelor's crap" prepared back in camp by Mrs. Smith!

After dinner, as we all gathered in the lounge, I offered a toast to Stuart, to honor his tireless efforts to keep the overland expedition going as smoothly as possible in the face of almost insurmountable challenges, both from group conflict and disastrous mechanical problems! As I hoisted my glass to toast Stuart, I felt he was a true friend, amazing coach driver, and a very warm, caring human being, in every sense of the word. My journey across Africa, and that of many others, had been made so much more memorable and rewarding because of Stuart! Thanks and appreciation can sometimes be difficult to express to a friend, but often the most sincere and meaningful.

Having concluded the evening, we made our way back to camp, and as I climbed into the tent, the night air was pleasantly cool, moist and filled with the sounds of animals and birds in the distance. In the dim moonlight, a small herd of wildebeest and zebra grazed quietly nearby.

The next morning, we arose early, before the night had a chance to leave our campsite. As we "puttered" around in the semi-darkness, the first rays of sunshine slowly made their way to our eyes—approaching like the first soft raindrops of an impending storm. As they gathered themselves into greater and brighter battalions, the surrounding landscape rose from its slumber to bid us welcome to the day. The dull greys and blacks became lighter and more complex, until silhouettes lost their outlines and expanded to take on familiar shapes and scenes. It was as if the rising sun, by its rays of early light, had put life back into the earth, much as a man might pump air into a balloon. It all happened so slowly and steadily; one could follow its drama moment by moment.

It was then that I became aware of the most awesome element that dominated the emerging landscape—a massive monolith crowned by a cap of pale pink. Mt Kilimanjaro slowly awoke to his reign over the plains of East Africa.

As the sun rose higher in the eastern sky, so too did the mountain seem to rise from the broad expanse below. Its crown of pale pink gradually transformed into brilliant, sparkling white through an endless number of shades.

Mt Kilimanjaro at sunrise – Amboseli National Park, Kenya

Such an amazing event deserved the flattery of a photograph, so I tried my best to capture a few moments in the life of the magnificent mountain with my camera. I took several photos of the mountain meeting the sunrise or was it the other way around. It was an awesome sight that would stay with me for a lifetime! There was no question that Mt Kilimanjaro dominated the land, as it had from time immemorial. Throughout the day, the mountain would accompany us wherever we went in the national park, to watch over us, and perhaps to remind us just how small we really were!

Before heading toward Nairobi, our elusive goal for the past four months, Stuart suggested one more tour of the park on our way out. There was a small lake just off the main road, and that particular morning, we chanced upon a lone Cheetah perched upon a small mound, staring at the mountain and being warmed by the sun. We were able to approach him at close quarters, and it was fascinating to watch as he groomed himself. In the end, he just seemed to brush us off as just another "annoyance". Further along the track, we came upon a large group of elephants, giraffe, and cape buffalo, before the cruel demon of misfortune struck, in the disguise of a long stretch of super slick mud! Suddenly, the old bus went skidding across the surface like it was on ice skates—twisting and turning, trying desperately to avoid the large thorn bushes. But alas, we crashed into a massive thorn bush and abruptly sputtered to a halt! The engine was dead and so was the battery—and in the worst possible place to push start a vehicle. But we had no choice, it was here or never, so we chose to try to push the old bus back out of the mud to a large patch of grass. As we strained for all we were worth, we finally managed to move the lumbering beast back onto the grass.

Our first few attempts to push start Kong were hopeless, the rear wheels just "skidded" on the wet grass and refused to turn over. Just as we were about to "throw in the towel" and walk back to the lodge, Krem suggested we try putting the bus in third gear. Sure enough, as a small patch of dry grass appeared beneath the wheels, the engine kicked over and began to roar out a loud apology to us. Quickly, we headed straight for the main road, paranoid of anything that remotely resembled mud. And so ended our stay in Amboseli National Park, still under the watchful eye of Mt Kilimanjaro. The mountain continued to keep vigilance over our old bus as we steadily drove toward Nairobi. Whenever I occasionally looked back at the mountain, I began to appreciate its importance in East Africa, and in some small way, I understood why it had become sacred, mysterious, and enchanting to the Maasai people—a noble and proud people living in the shadow of a noble and proud mountain. At that moment, I vowed to return to Mt Kilimanjaro and scale its lofty heights, in search of a personal reward—a gift for my soul!

CHAPTER SEVEN

January 2, 1975
Nairobi, Kenya

"*The City at Last*" Finally, we were just a few miles from Nairobi, and as we glimpsed the city's skyline on the horizon for the first time, we were sure it would fulfill all the fantasies of which we had dreamed throughout the arduous journey across the continent. Kong was running quite well, trundling down the tarmac at 30 mph. But in the back of everyone's mind, though never spoken aloud, was a fear, and somehow a perverted expectation of one more visit from the ghost of mechanical failures! I felt it took some real nerve and lots of faith on the part of Stuart, to stay at the wheel of the old bus. As we neared the edge of Nairobi, more and more buildings appeared, lots of people walking alongside the road, and a modern railway track accompanied us into the city. More traffic bid us welcome as well, and just then, rising before us were several tall, high-rise buildings—a "vision" like that of Cortez seeking the seven cities of gold! It was as if a small-scale version of New York City had suddenly sprung up from the vast plains of East Africa—a fountain of gold from a deep well. It actually took us another 30 minutes to reach the heart of the city, but that mattered not, for we had the skyline in our sight the entire time.

As we drove into the city center, it felt like a brand-new experience, when compared to entering the hundreds of small villages we had encountered on our long journey across Africa. Visions of the post office and long-awaited news from home filled our minds as Stuart parked the old bus on Kenyatta Avenue, Nairobi's main street. We all dashed across the road to the post office in search of mail, and fortunately, there were letters for everyone, including my dear Marion who had been out of contact with her home since the beginning of September! Besides the most welcome letters from family and friends, I received one from a stranger in Seattle, requesting my evaluation of SIAFU Overland Expeditions. My response would be tempered from four months of difficult and challenging life experiences. Once we had read our letters, we climbed back aboard King Kong for the final leg of our journey, a short distance to "City Park"—a campground near the center of town where overland groups camped.

We were making our way down Nairobi's busiest thoroughfare, when the perennial "Ghost of Mechanical Mischief" paid us one final visit to "throw a wrench in the works"! The old beast sputtered, coughed a couple of times, and then died in the middle of the busy street - King Kong had finally given up, it was his last breath! As we sat helpless in the heavy traffic, the irony and mad satire of the situation was a fitting and well-deserved climax to our harrowing journey across Africa. As Bartie put it so eloquently, "we all knew it was bound to happen"—no truer words were ever spoken. As some local men on the street helped push us to the side of the road, we forgot our embarrassment and burst out laughing at the whole fucking mess—what a cruel joke had been played upon us! Had the "ghost" been responsible, or perhaps we had all chosen the wrong time to make the journey across Africa? While some people could easily lay the blame on SIAFU, and in particular the old bus named King Kong, I knew, as well as Stuart, Kong had done his best to overcome the mechanical challenges, in order to fulfill his commitment to get us safely to Nairobi. At that moment, I realized, over the course of the past four months, I had developed a deep respect for Stuart and a strong bond with King Kong.

Finally, we arrived at City Park, set up our tents, gathered together our gear, and then waited for something else to happen—which it did shortly afterwards. The local SIAFU manager arrived with loads of fresh meat and vegetables, along with stacks of more mail. It was a very nice surprise, and then he invited us to stay at a private estate, with much nicer facilities, in the hills outside of town—"would we like to move there"? We all thought about it for a few seconds and replied, "by all means"! But as expected, Seymour and the Smiths wanted to decline the offer—we would just as soon have left them camped there. However, as we began pulling up camp and loading gear on another truck, they eventually came with us, mumbling and grumbling the whole way.

The private estate turned out to be quite a long way out of the city center, in an exclusive European section. We had the use of hot showers for the first time in weeks, as well as a real, genuine bathtub—very soothing for aching muscles and sore bones. A delicious dinner of steak and potatoes soon followed, along with a soft, quiet feeling of relief that we had finally arrived in Nairobi—the end of an epic journey! As the evening waned, thoughts of future plans began to play in our minds. We had made it to Nairobi all right, with a lot of great driving, strong determination, lots of help along the way, and also a bit of luck some-times. As I shared a cold bottle of local Tusker beer with Stuart, the trip was already beginning to "mellow" a bit around the edges—the advantage of having the perspective of time. Eventually came the question that each of us would have to ponder—what to do and where to go now? It was a question that John and I discussed as well—to remain in Nairobi, travel to new destinations, or perhaps return home? The next few days would determine the answer!

January 3-10, 1974
Nairobi, Kenya

"Nairobi—Back to Civilization" The next day, as I expected, John had done a marvelous job of booking accommodations in advance - a room for $1.50 a night at a very nice little Indian rest house, not far from the city center. It was another example of his unofficial, yet stylized role as our tour guide. He and I loaded our gear into a private car provided by SIAFU, and soon arrived at the "Hill Station Lodge", for an indefinite period of time.

Room #3 - Hill Station Lodge, Nairobi

At last I felt as if we had "settled" down somewhere we could call home for a while—no longer on an endless journey. We checked into a neat little room for two—very clean and tidy, and complete with breakfast. Once we had stowed our stuff and arranged for our clothes to be washed, we walked up toward the city center to take a short tour of what Nairobi might have to offer.

One of the first places to catch our eye was the "Thorn Tree Café" in the famous New Stanley Hotel downtown. Later, it would become the "mecca" to meet other Overlanders around noon each day. It soon became the place where we would always see people we knew, even if we hadn't arranged a time to meet, and the most important spot for all of us while we were in Nairobi. After a quick tour of the hotel, and the purchase of the latest Time Magazine from the corner newsstand, I headed for the nearest Barclay's Bank, of which there must have been 20 branches downtown. There I was able to pick up $960 in traveler's checks that my dear friend Joan had been kind enough to wire from my bank in Seattle. To my surprise and great delight, the transaction took less than 20 minutes! I was in and out "in a flash", so to speak. From the bank, I went to meet up with John at the Thorn Tree Café where we had lunch and coffee together.

I spent the afternoon shopping downtown, mainly in bookstores and music shops. I discovered a small record shop where the owner would record the music from any of his records on to cassette tapes. Despite the rather limited selection of music, I had a lot of fun browsing through all the records and selecting some for recording on tape. Later that afternoon, I had a fantastic time perusing through a couple of bookstores, and what struck me was the fact that all the books were in English! (I had gotten used to hearing and seeing the French language during most of the trip.) Being in Nairobi at last, I felt reassured familiar things were still available. As evening approached, I met up with John again at the New Stanley Hotel (NSH) where we discussed options for dinner. At long last, we now had the opportunity to choose among a vast array of foods, not being stuck with a mere five choices of dehydrated rations! As we contemplated a number of different cuisines, it turned out both of us were looking forward to some Chinese food.

So off we went, in search of a place called "Mandarin Restaurant", having been recommended by another Overlander at a nearby table in the Thorn Tree Café. We found the restaurant to be very nice and with a wide selection of dishes. However, the tall black waiters seemed a bit out of place, although they were very friendly and anxious to serve us. Still, there was some difficulty in understanding our order, so we resorted to pointing at the menu—one from column A and two from column B. When our food arrived, we were not disappointed—it was a superb dinner! After which we "strolled" around the Indian section of the city in search of some evening entertainment. At first glance, it appeared there were no bars or clubs around, since we could see no neon signs, flashing lights, or music to be heard. But just as we rounded a corner, there it was—"Club Fantastic", and it was "jumping" to the sounds of loud African pop!

Right away, John picked up on it and said, "it's the Zaire beat", and I had to agree it was the same as we had heard in Kisangani several weeks before. As we climbed the stairs to the second floor, from which the heavy vibrations were emanating, we passed several drunken men being lead downstairs from the third floor by giggling young ladies. It was pretty clear what kind of "shenanigans" were going on upstairs! The club was very crowded and cost us 5 schillings to get in to see the action, of which there was plenty. John and I quickly decided we weren't quite up to bouncing around the dance floor like bumper cars, so we retired to a quiet table in a small corner to have a cold beer. Just as we sat down and ordered the beer, a couple of young black guys came to our table and began their "welcome stranger" rap, as though to hustle us for a beer. But as time went on, we realized we were quite the objects of attention—I suspected it must have been "cool" for them to be seen talking with us! As I looked around the club, I could see no other white folks, so I was pretty sure very few whites ever ventured into Club Fantastic!

One of the guys in particular, who was well on his way to oblivion, kept talking to us, often repeating himself. John and I got the feeling he was just waiting for us to buy him a beer, but we didn't make the offer. After a half hour he left, and we thought we were finally rid of him. However, a short time later, he returned with a friend, and to our astonishment, he bought us a couple of beers, though we really didn't need them at that point in the evening. But by that time, we were obligated to listen to his bullshit, which turned out to be some racist slander about the Kikuyu people being the best, strongest, and most intelligent in Kenya— blah, blah, blah! At one point he stopped for a moment, and then said, "when President Kenyatta dies, there will be civil war"! It was a very sobering statement that gave us quite a shock! We endured his bullshit for as long as possible and then made our move to leave the club. Just then, our new "friend" insisted we come to the movie theatre where he worked, to see the new Jimi Hendricks film, with his compliments. We thanked him for his generous hospitality and finally rolled out of the club around 1:00am in the morning. As we went down the stairs, we passed a steady stream of young ladies with gentlemen in tow, on their way up to the third floor. So went the first day on our own in Nairobi!

Our second day in the city was much like the first, and the third much like the first two, and so on. A routine was quickly being established as we settled in. On the evening of the third day, Ginny and Marion joined us at the Hill Station Lodge, which added immensely to our experience exploring Nairobi—we quickly became a foursome. Our typical day began around 8:00am with breakfast consisting of an egg, toast, butter, jam, banana, and a cup of hot tea. Though the breakfast menu never varied, it was tasty and a good start to our day. Breakfast was always served by a little old Indian man who was as quiet and as soft spoken as a "dormouse"! Following our leisurely breakfast, it was time for a shower, and perhaps a bit of reading and writing before we made our way up to the center of town to do some shopping. We would usually meet up again at the Thorn Tree Café around 11:00am for coffee, then to the Post Office to check for letters from home, before going to lunch. The choices for lunch included the "Honey Pot", "Lamu Restaurant", and the "New Avenue Hotel", which was famous for its huge "all you could eat" salad buffet. At only 6 schillings, it was truly a remarkable bargain! After lunch, we usually spent the afternoon browsing through the numerous stores and shops downtown, including a stop for coffee and Danish pastries at the "Bachelor's Bakery". About 4:00pm, it was time for tea at the Thorn Tree Café, after which we strolled back to the Hill Station Lodge to rest and freshen up for dinner—and a chance to add some spice to our day.

One evening, the four of us went to a local Indian restaurant around the corner called the "Supreme Hotel". ("hotel" in Africa often referred to nothing more than a proper restaurant, as opposed to a simple corner shop or kiosk) The restaurant had a fantastic collection of exotic, mysterious, and intriguing smells that were sometimes sweet, pungent, hot, spicy, and fragrant—all in one! Inside was a large glass display case of sweet pastries, cakes, and candies in some of the strangest shapes, colors, and textures. We sampled many of them and they were delicious. Almost all of them were made with honey and other exotic natural sweeteners, rather than sugar or artificial flavorings. All of the dishes on the menu were vegetarian and an incredible array of flavors and fragrances. The variety of spices, sauces, and vegetables was amazing! Not only was the food a delight for our taste buds, it was very inexpensive.

Another evening, we decided to try a local steakhouse near the NSH, for what we anticipated to be an expensive, so-so meal, but it would be a change from our usual diet. As it turned out that evening, we savored some of the best steaks we had ever tasted in our life! My steak was so tender it could be cut with a fork. The garlic cream sauce that accompanied the steak was absolutely delicious. But the biggest shock of the evening came when we were presented with the bill—the whole dinner cost each of us just a mere 15 schillings, about $2.00! On another occasion, we had dinner at a tiny local northern Indian restaurant that served some very tasty charcoal grilled shish kebab and spicy chicken. It soon became a favorite eatery and notable for one of its specialties on the menu that caused considerable confusion.

One evening, Krem and I saw "eggroll" on the menu and decided to order one, all the while visualizing something resembling the classic Chinese version. But when it arrived at our table, it was a strange sight to behold! We all looked at the dish with amazement and disbelief—on the plate before us was a "hot dog bun" with slices of hard-boiled egg stuck inside, and nothing else! We all stared at it in silence for a few seconds, and then burst out in raucous laughter, much to the embarrassment of the young black waiters. What kind of cruel joke had been played upon us?

A couple of days later, John got the itch to move on again, and decided to travel down to the coastal town of Mombasa, in order to "scout" out the city for us. As he left Nairobi that evening, Ginny, Marion and I chose to try another oriental restaurant called the "Bamboo Shoot". It was a beautiful place with a quiet atmosphere, very friendly service, and a wide variety of delicious dishes from China, Indonesia, Malaysia, and India. With great gastronomic pleasure, the three of us ordered eight different items and literally stuffed ourselves that night. I thought it was more than enough to satiate the appetite of most men, let alone two females. But, to my surprise, they were still hungry as we left the restaurant.

So off we went, tromping around downtown Nairobi at 11pm, in search of more food. The first stop was at the "Honey Pot" for coffee, sandwiches, and ice cream bars! Then it was on to the Thorn Tree Café, one of the few places still open at that late hour. I sat in disbelief as Ginny and Marion literally inhaled a plate of chocolate eclairs, followed by an order of "Welsh Rarebit"! At that moment, I began to become a bit paranoid whenever I looked into their eyes—all I saw was the look of starvation! If there had been a McDonald's or 7/11 store nearby, I was certain they would have beaten a fast path to it. Eventually we ended up back at the Hill Station Lodge and a welcome night of rest.

Besides always being on a "food trip", or so it seemed during our first few days in Nairobi, we managed to find a few entertainment spots of interest. Being that most of the establishments with any decent music for dancing were the large tourist hotels, where one had to sport a measure of wealth beyond our means, not counting the Club Fantastic, we resorted to the cinema one evening. The film was a rather mediocre James Bond type thriller that turned out to be a sad satire, complete with "silly" clichés depicting the obvious lack of intelligence on the part of the film's hero. But we all enjoyed it for the laughter and comedy, though most unintentional.

Our other venture into evening entertainment in Nairobi took us to the National Theatre. After some haggling about membership and ticket prices, we were able to watch the play titled "Doctor in the House". It was a delightful English comedy about a group of young medical students sharing a house together. The theatre was very nice, with an intimate setting, and we had a marvelous time. The experience was very refreshing and stimulating—and brought back memories of the many times I had attended plays at the Empty Space Theatre and Repertory Theatre in Seattle. I loved the lively presence and spontaneity of live performances, and I realized how much I had missed that sort of cultural experience traveling across Africa.

On another evening, an especially memorable and meaningful one, Stuart invited us to a dinner party in my honor, as a way of saying thanks for the help I had given him during all the mechanical breakdowns on the trip. To be honest, I enjoyed helping with the repairs to the old bus, much more so than sitting helplessly on the side of the road with the rest of the group. Although I wasn't expecting it, I appreciated his thank you celebration very much! Stuart was a very warm and sensitive person whom I valued as a good friend. So, his expression of thanks meant a great deal to me. His friendship kept me going on many occasions when I might otherwise have just as easily split from the trip, as so many others had done along the way. And then there was my developing relationship with Marion that became a strong reason for remaining on the trip. (and little did I know then how it would change my life forever)

And, so went our time in Nairobi as we slowly "decompressed" from the long, arduous journey across Africa with SIAFU and King Kong. Now we were on our own, with no timeline, schedule, or obligations. A couple days earlier, John had decided to head down to Mombasa on the coast of the Indian Ocean. We were confident he would do a superb job of scouting out places to stay, things to see, and people to meet. We would meet up with him in Mombasa and then discuss future travel options.

On our last night in Nairobi, Ginny, Marion, and I went back to the Bamboo Shoot a delicious Chinese meal that filled us to the brim. No sooner had we walked out of the restaurant than Ginny insisted we walk over to the "Iceland Milk Bar" for coffee and pastries, which seemed harmless enough. However, once we got there, the two of them began ordering toasted cheese sandwiches and milk shakes! As we left the milk bar, we hadn't walked two blocks before Marion insisted that we go to the Thorn Tree Café to see if anyone we knew was there. Of course, this was just another excuse to order more food, in the form of pastries and sandwiches. I just sat in disbelief—it was a farewell to Nairobi in a blaze of gastronomic glory!

January 11-12, 1975
Nairobi to Mombasa

"Midnight Bus to Mombasa" The next morning, we packed our things and prepared to leave Nairobi. We had heard from many Overlanders that the bus was the most economical mode of transportation to Mombasa. So, I enquired of the departure times and found a bus scheduled to leave Nairobi at 8:30pm, arriving in Mombasa at 6:00am the next morning. It seemed to be a reasonable schedule and the price was right, so I bought three tickets. We spent our last day in typical Nairobi style, "lounging" from one coffee house to another, and from one shop to another, until the hour of departure approached. We picked up our bags at the Hill Station Lodge and trudged over to "East African Road Services" in search of our bus to Mombasa. What we found was at least 25 buses and

hundreds of people scrambling to board them, carrying everything from bulging cardboard boxes to crates of chickens—it was insane! With all the buses looking alike, which bus did we have tickets for?

Finally, amid the confusion and chaos, I spotted someone who looked like he worked for East African Road Services, and he directed us to one of the buses. Then, having shown our tickets to someone standing beside the bus, wearing a faded green uniform, we were pushed aboard. As I looked down the aisle, the bus was totally full! But just then, he "evicted" people from three seats and bid us to be seated. As we sat in our "assigned" seats, the mass chaos and confusion continued for another half hour, while people kept shuffling among the seats in the bus. It seemed no one really knew if they were in the right seat or not! Pandemonium reigned right up to the last minute, with people jumping on and off the bus as it pulled out of the parking lot. At that point, I could only hope we were on a bus going to Mombasa!

At last, we were on our way, bouncing along the highway, with the three of us squeezed into some pretty hard, very uncomfortable seats. Soon, the lights in the bus were turned off and we began an attempt to catch a bit of sleep, constantly squirming and shifting, trying to find a position that was halfway comfortable for three people. It was a very difficult task which took the better part of the 10-hour journey. As we would doze off for a few minutes, the bus would keep stopping at every nook and cranny along the road. And every time the bus stopped, there was a constant maneuvering of people to either get on or off. It became "jungle rules"—every man, woman, and child for himself! As I watched the chaotic scene repeat itself again and again, I wondered why Africans had to do everything the hard way? Amid all the passengers entering and exiting the bus, was a group of vendors hawking everything from newspapers and coconuts to Fanta soda and boiled eggs—what a mess! I managed to buy some bananas and boiled eggs without losing my seat, luckily.

Suddenly, in the midst of the mad scramble, the bus began to move and the chaotic scene of people hopping on or off the bus was reenacted once again for the umpteenth time! Eventually, for what seemed like forever and a distance halfway across Africa, the bus rolled into Mombasa very early in the morning. Then, the same bus station madness happened all over again.

Once the three of us had managed to get off the bus, we sat down to one side and watched the crowd battle for their baggage piled high on the roof of the bus. At last, we claimed our bags, the only ones left. We had the name of the place where John was to be staying in Mombasa, but no idea of its location. I enquired at the bus station, but no one knew of the "Cozy Guest House". Finally, a taxi driver said he knew of it and would take us there. So, we piled into his dilapidated old car with all our bags.

Once he got the old beast started, he drove down the street and pulled into a service station to ask directions! That was when my suspicions were aroused. Even the service station attendant didn't know, so we roared off down the street to a tiny Chinese restaurant, where once again our driver asked for directions! Confident now that he knew it location, we drove back to the main street and promptly passed right by the "Cozy Guest House". Immediately, I pointed to it, whereupon he put the old car in reverse and backed up to the front door. As I looked around, I realized where we were—just two blocks from the bus station! The whole episode had cost us 5 schillings, a definite "rip-off". Anxiously, we climbed the stairs of the Cozy Guest House to meet up with John, who we figured must still be in bed at such an early hour on Sunday morning. Instead, we found a note from him to say he had moved across the street to the "Visitor's Inn" and had reserved two double rooms for all of us. So, we bid farewell to the Cozy Guest House and hauled our gear across the street.

When we checked with the Visitor's Inn, we were told he had not shown up that night, which caused us some concern. Rather than commit ourselves to the room reservations without discussing plans with John first, we left our stuff with the front desk and went in search of some coffee. After a few "bum" leads as to what places might be open at 6:00am on Sunday, we ended up walking the streets and sitting in the park for two hours. Upon returning to the Visitor's Inn, there was still no sign of John. By that time, we were tired and frustrated, having no place to hang out and wait for John. We finally talked the front desk clerk into giving us access to John's room, where we could at least lie down to rest after the miserable "Midnight Ride" and Sunday morning stroll. As we entered the room, we instantly recognized it as John's—his stuff was strewn everywhere, scattered to the winds in apparent abandonment! We settled down to washing up a bit and tried to get a few winks of sleep.

Then suddenly, the door flung open and John burst into the room, looking very embarrassed and guilty. We knew something was amiss by his heavily bandaged, blood stained finger. Slowly, the story emerged about his previous night's escapade with an "exotic" lady, which had ended up in a vicious fight over money. During the encounter, where John tried to recover his eyeglasses, the "lady of the night" chomped on his finger, taking quite a healthy bite. That was quite unacceptable to John, not to mention being very painful. Some of the other girls in the house managed to do a bit of first aid and sent him on his way! It could have been a rather funny story, but it was a painful and embarrassing one for John. To make things worse, we found out later that he had lost $50 in cash to a con man the day before, on the pretense of exchanging it on the black market. So, after listening to the accounts of John's adventures, we all decided to spend a couple more days in Mombasa.

Then we went about resting in the room for the day, trying to beat the oppressive heat and humidity. That evening, the four of us went out to dinner at a very nice Indian restaurant called the "Curry Bowl" for some delicious seafood. Following a leisurely dinner, we walked around the old quarter of the city, where the Arabic influence was most pronounced. The dark, narrow streets were filled with small groups of people drinking coffee and engaged in lively conversation by lamplight—the scene was very exotic and quaint! We ended the evening with a cup of coffee in a tiny café, before walking back to the Visitor's Inn, in the glow of a full moon.

January 13, 1975
Mombasa, Kenya

"On the Coast of the Indian Ocean" After the typical breakfast of an egg, toast, jam, banana, and hot tea, we began discussing John's idea of renting a beach cottage somewhere on the coast of the Indian Ocean for an extended stay. We all agreed it was a fantastic idea, so John and I volunteered to check with a company named "Fourways Accommodations", while Ginny and Marion shopped for some food in a local market. During their shopping trip, they discovered a marvelous little bakery that had lovely fresh bread, pastries, and cookies. Marion bought a kilo of assorted cookies, which turned out to be delicious and very popular. Later, we all met up at the Visitor's Inn and John said he had heard a lot of great things about the island of Lamu off the coast of Kenya, south of Somalia. It was supposed to be a very beautiful place that few tourists ever visited, which sounded great to us.

So, we made arrangements to rent a two-bedroom furnished house on the island. Then, the only thing left to do was to buy bus tickets to Lamu Island. That evening, we packed our bags in order to be prepared to leave early the next morning and made ready for any early bedtime. But lo and behold, it was not to be, since John had purchased a bottle of gin and Krem happened to show up! As the night went on, John, Ginny and Krem got pretty drunk—meanwhile, Marion and I occupied ourselves with each other's company. Finally, everyone's eyelids became too heavy, and the realization of an early morning departure spurred everyone to seek sleep!

January 14, 1975
Mombasa to Lamu Island

"The Seven Hour Chant" We arose early the next morning in great anticipation of our impending journey north to Lamu Island. After a quick breakfast, we hiked over to the "Tawakal Bus Company" to board

the bus. Once again, it was the usual confusion and chaos, as we had experienced in Nairobi. Everyone and his brother were trying to get on the bus at the same time, carrying overloaded cardboard boxes and huge, bulging plastic bags—but no crates of chickens, thank goodness. We had no choice but to do the same— so, we pushed and shoved our way onto the bus, after having gotten our bags up on to the roof of the bus. Once we had finally found some seats, there was the inevitable wait for something to happen, which always turned out to be nothing in the end.

As we sat inside the hot stuffy bus, we watched a constant shuffle of people getting on and off the crowded bus. The seats were just as hard and uncomfortable as those on the "Midnight Ride" from Nairobi to Mombasa. When I looked around, everyone except the four of us was black and Muslim. I noticed all of the men wore long skirts and small round hats made of beautifully embroidered white cloth. The women were dressed in long black outer garments, known as "Chador", that covered them from head to toe, and occasionally with a veil as well. I began to get a sense of the strong influence of the Arabic culture along the coast of East Africa, which had existed for hundreds of years—preserved in the religion, dress, architecture and local customs. It was abundantly clear we were now surrounded by it very intriguing and exotic.

Suddenly, as if on the whim of the driver, the bus roared away from the station and on to the main highway—the start of our long journey to Lamu. We hadn't gone more than a few miles before a loud- speaker directly above our heads began to blare out the shrill, ear piercing voice of a man chanting verses from the Holy Quran. At first, it just seemed as though his voice was constantly off-key and possessed of a strong nasal tone—loud and unintelligible. But as the hours wore on, it became painful and torturous. Hour after hour, mile after dusty mile, his tributes to Allah continued to "blast" forth above our heads and straight through our eardrums. It rapidly became oppressive, monotonous, and was always unwavering in volume—full blast! It seemed nothing could distract my attention from the continuous chanting, no matter how hard I tried. I didn't know about the Muslims on the bus, but I felt I was being tortured for something I had done to offend Allah, yet I had no idea what it could be, nor could I "submit" to anyone in order to stop it.

On and on, the dusty miles of dirt road lay before us, and the chanting seemed as endless as the road ahead. At that point, I that felt the man chanting verses was quite capable of outlasting us by a great distance! And then, as had happened so many times on our trip across Africa, when we had felt we were on the edge of losing our minds, the chanting came to an abrupt end! For a few moments, the echoes continued to fill our heads, our ears still "ringing". The bus had arrived at the end of the road and the motor sputtered to a halt. We sat in disbelief—we had survived the full force of the chants, amid a hundred miles of dust, potholes, and stifling heat. We got off the bus and managed to grab our bags from the roof. It was a short walk to the dock, where we stood among the crowd waiting to board the small boat to Lamu Island.

Following seven hours of ear-splitting chants, the four of us were looking forward to finding a great measure of peace and quiet on the island. It almost seemed like, by the bus ride, we had somehow passed a "test" to be allowed to enter the peace and serenity of Lamu Island. But, before we could enter that realm, we had to endure the scene of chaos and confusion on the dock, an experience that had become all too familiar. As the crowd attempted to scramble aboard the boat, I began to wonder, why use two boats when one boat could be overloaded instead? Every inch of space was piled high with human flesh, cardboard boxes, bulging plastic bags, chickens, dogs, and almost anything else people could carry. I looked around at that point and figured the boat could hold no more, but how wrong I was—another 10 people climbed over us to perch on anything that resembled a boat. Finally, as the boat pulled away from the dock, it rode so low in the water that waves began to wash over the side.

Thankfully, it was a relatively short voyage to Lamu town. (during the trip, I wondered what it must be like in a storm? When at last we reached the island, another scene of chaos "welcomed" us. As the boat slowly approached the dock, people on our overcrowded boat attempted to jump onto the dock, without falling in the water, while at the same time, people on the dock tried to jump on to the boat. It quickly became almost a "stalemate" of two equal and opposing forces. It was all I could do to get ashore and act as a "relay" for our baggage. We managed to force our way onto the dock without losing anyone or our gear. It was simply a case of having to be as forceful and pushy as the Africans, otherwise we could have been trampled.

At last, as we stood on the waterfront and the chaos slowly faded away, we began to feel the peace and quiet of the island—a fabled Arab isle of tranquility. We found the owner of the house we had rented, a wealthy Indian merchant with a profitable real estate and jewelry business on the island. He handed us the keys to the house and gave us directions to it, supposedly a 15-minute walk down the beach. Actually, it was closer to 30 minutes, but when we arrived, we discovered a gorgeous, white-washed Indian style house on the beach, just a few yards from the ocean.

Our house on Lamu Island, Kenya

And behind the house was an area of large sand dunes and palm trees. Better yet, there was not another house in sight!

We rushed inside to survey the premises. Though it was sparsely furnished, it was very comfortable. Most of the furniture was quite modern, largely plastic and metal. But the beds were made of beautifully carved tropical wood, with a frame of cane stretched across it to form the "bed springs". On top of the bed frame was a thick foam mattress covered in bright fabric. One unique feature of the bed was its height, being almost as high as the dining room table! It was no exaggeration to say we had *to literally "climb into bed"*. Once we had settled into our new "home", we immediately changed into cutoff shorts and sandals, which would become our daily wear on Lamu Island. Then we all ran outside to our own beach for a swim in the Indian Ocean. The water was clear blue and pleasantly warm, though the sun was quite hot and intense. (during our time on Lamu Island, we had to take precautions every day to avoid sunburn

The first evening, as the sun slowly set behind the sand dunes, and the warm ocean breeze filled our house with the soft sound of waves caressing the beach, we knew we had found paradise! The sound of the ocean waves continued into the night, providing us with a peaceful setting for our most needed slumber. That evening ushered in the beginning of an incredible, magical experience! We had discovered paradise for sure.

January 15–February 3, 1975
Lamu Island, Kenya

"A Day on Lamu Island" A day on Lamu Island was like a day in a "time machine" set for the 18th century. The town of Lamu was old and weathered, stretching along the sea wall and waterfront. The buildings were of classic Arabic and Indian architecture, and the abundance of palm trees gave the town a distinctive tropical atmosphere. It was quaint without being touristy or pretentious, and the vast majority of people on the island were long-time residents. The waterfront was always a buzz of activity and the center of commerce.

Lamu town waterfront - Kenya

A long stone sea wall formed the base, with several old wooden docks and a front street of sand where only foot traffic and donkeys were pe mitted. In fact, there were no cars or trucks on the entire island.

Each day, boats would come and go, with many anchored in the small harbor. Just up the hill from the waterfront was the second "main" street, and like all the streets in Lamu town, it was a very narrow cobblestone passageway separating the front doors of the adjacent buildings. As a "street", by normal definition, it hardly qualified. But since there were no motorized vehicles on the island, it only had to serve foot traffic, which it did with a great deal of lively activity.

Activity on the streets of Lamu town

Most of the streets in the center of town were lined with an endless number of small shops, selling everything from soup to nuts. Now and then, there were also small restaurants serving local dishes, along with many small food stands and vendors offering fresh fruit juices, tea, and specialty foods. No matter how many times I walked down the streets of Lamu town, it continued to amaze me how all the shops managed to stay in business, selling pretty much the same things at the same prices! Somehow, by the look of them, I could tell they had all been there a long time—perhaps in their family for generations. In some places, the streets were just wide enough for two people to pass, and often with an open drain on one side.

At night, it got quite dark and a bit eerie in the glow of kerosene lanterns and burning candles. But it wasn't long before we came to realize that crime on the island was almost unheard of. In the center of town was a small square with a massive stone building on one side. There was a small tower on each corner of the building and a long flight of steps

146

leading up to a huge, intricately carved wooden door. (beautifully old carved wooden doors were especially unique to Lamu and could be seen everywhere on the island) But this particular imposing building overlooking the square happened to be the local jail! And every morning, the prisoners were marched out to do manual labor around town, then back to their cells in the evening. Watching this daily "ceremony" a few times, I came to the conclusion that it was arranged to impress everyone with the consequences of crime.

Meanwhile, the streets of Lamu town bustled with the daily business of buying and selling—a kind of social activity.

Typical "street" in Lamu town

During the afternoons and evenings, small groups of men would sit outside small cafes drinking tea or coffee and discussing the important issues of the day—at least those of importance to someone, though I was never sure of the issue or to whom it was important. Each day, someone from our group was likely to walk into town to buy some staples, like butter, bread, eggs, jam and tea. We quickly gained a local shopper's knowledge of which shops had the best foods at the cheapest prices.

After a while, we became familiar faces at some of our favorite shops and began receiving special attention. It worked well in our favor and cut down on the time needed for shopping trips. It was soon after that we established a shopping routine—be at the fish market before 11:00am for the freshest seafood, fresh baked bread at 2:00pm, shops closed at 1:00pm for lunch, and the "New Star Restaurant" had the least expensive lunch menu.

Ray with staff of New Star Restaurant, Lamu town

Marion and I preferred to spend much of our time together at the house or on the beach, rather than going into town every day. Fortunately, John and Ginny enjoyed the shopping trips, so there was never a problem in maintaining a constant supply of food each day.

A few days after we arrived, some local fishermen stopped by the house to sell us fresh fish, crab, and lobster they had caught in the morning. Everything they offered was incredibly inexpensive and amazingly good. Large crabs cost us about 3 schillings each, lobsters for 10 schillings a kilo, and a huge rock cod or sea bass was 20–25 schillings. (a Kenyan Schilling was the equivalent of 20 cents at the time) We ate virtually nothing but seafood the entire time we were on the island! We prepared everything from crab and lobster omelets, to fish chowder, charcoal grilled fish, and spaghetti with lobster sauce. Every one of our meals was like a gourmet dinner, including the trimmings and side salads of fresh produce and fruit.

The most memorable meals were dinners on the veranda, with beautiful music, under moonlight reflected off the ocean, and caressed by a soft, cool evening breeze! Our veranda was simply one of the most beautiful places anywhere in the world to enjoy the bounty of the sea. I don't think even the finest restaurants in the world could have surpassed the peaceful atmosphere and relaxing experience of our dinners on the veranda! Only the soft breeze through the palm trees broke the silence of the evening. We always looked forward to dinners on the veranda, and soon began to share the experience with guests from among our fellow travelers in Lamu town. On those occasions, we always followed dinner with coffee and quiet conversation on the veranda as the tide came in, the waves played with the beach, and the wind softly brushed the palm trees. It always made a perfect ending to another beautiful day on Lamu Island!

Every day was a beautiful day at our house and usually began very early, with the sunrise that streamed through our bedroom window. Then it was time for tea and coffee on the veranda before breakfast.

Marion with her morning coffee - Lamu Island

Sometimes we also took a dip in the ocean, before sitting down to a delicious crab or lobster omelet, together with fresh pineapple and mango. After breakfast, we either made preparations to go into town to do some shopping, or settled down to reading, writing, or sunbathing. Often, especially in the afternoon, we would walk around the eastern tip of the island, past the small fishing village of Shella, to a long expanse of beautiful white sand beach on the other side of the island that extended in a huge arc along its entire length. Rarely did we see anyone on the beach, and the people we did see were a few travelers from Lamu town who often sunbathed in the nude.

At other times, we would walk to the beach on the other side of the island following a footpath through the huge sand dunes behind the house. The dunes were partially stabilized in many areas by dune grasses and small shrubs, but there were also large expanses of pure white sand that stretched all the way down to the beach. There was an area in the middle of the dunes with a small grove of coconut palms, which gave it the appearance of being in the middle of the Sahara Desert, especially since the area was often very hot with little movement of the air. I found the dunes to be particularly beautiful, but a bit eerie at night under the glow of a full moon, when the shrubs took on strange shapes and the white sand reflected some pretty weird shadows!

One night I remembered well, I walked through the dunes alone and had the feeling a thousand eyes were watching my every movement! And as I walked across the white sand, I had the illusion of being on a treadmill—there were very few reference points to measure my progress. At times it seemed like my mind played tricks on itself. When I finally reached the beach, massive waves rolled in and I could see whitecaps and foam as the waves crashed on the beach. My perspective of time and distance became warped out of proportion, and all I could really be sure about was that I was surrounded by the soft touch of white sand, the roar of the surf, and the bright light of the full moon. At that moment, I felt so in touch with nature that I took off my clothes and walked naked on the beach, while the waves washed over my feet in rhythm with the movement of the earth. The feeling that night was so personal and powerful, it has remained locked in my memory for a lifetime!

So, as the time passed, our days on Lamu Island were spent relaxing and enjoying life in the timeless world of beautiful beaches, exotic culture, and fascinating history. The sun was always full and intense from mid-morning until late afternoon, and it didn't take long before all of us were as brown as could be. During the heat of the day, it wasn't possible to lay out in the open for more than 15 or 20 minutes at a time. It was then that I retreated to the cool sanctuary of an ice-cold Tusker beer from the fridge! There was little time for boredom, though all our activities were conducted at a slower pace. John was probably more restless than the rest of us, and consequently, he spent more time in Lamu town, visiting with people we had met on the island, mostly in the evenings at "Petley's Inn".

As for me and Marion, we kept each other company a great deal of the time, often spending much of the day sunning ourselves, strolling down the beach, or walking through the dunes in the evening. Upon returning to the house, we would fix tea, take a shower, and then leisurely massage each other with lovely scented oil. It was always the most relaxing and sensuous moment of the day on Lamu Island! By then we were certainly in the mood for a quiet dinner under moonlight on the veranda. With each passing day, our love grew deeper and more intense—we formed a real and enduring bond, which I hoped would stand the test of time. And I knew it would be very difficult to leave the island when that time would eventually arrive. But, until then, we savored every moment we spent on the island of Lamu.

"Company's a Comin" During our first few days on the island, we met several fellow travelers who had come to Lamu for the same reasons as we had. We quickly formed friendships with many of them. There was Nicky, a young girl from Canada who was going to join the next SIAFU trip returning to London. And Robert, who was very much into photography and had worked for a short time with the government of Zaire. Then there was Seth, a young guy with a big smile and a warm heart, who was determined to go to Zaire and live with the Pygmies! Charles was a free spirit who was just "bumming" around Africa, with no itinerary or travel schedule. (he and John were kindred spirits Finally, there was Ray, an interesting young American who loved music, theatre, and all the arts.

About a week after we had arrived in Lamu, John and Ginny set about organizing our first dinner party. It turned out to be vegetarian because there was no fish available that day. We were also a bit short of plates and utensils, but dinner was a great success none the less. Everyone raved about the food, especially Marion's potato salad. We served dinner outside on the veranda, in the soft light of a full moon, and listened to music on my cassette tape player. After dinner, we had coffee and listened to Robert as he played his beautiful "Guild" guitar. His repertoire of traditional Mississippi blues was amazing, as well as his renditions of Leo Kottke songs, which were difficult for most musicians to play. Then he passed the guitar to Ray and we enjoyed some excellent Chicago jazz and blues music. The evening was one to remember! I laid back and listened to the mellow sound of the guitar—the veranda was acoustically perfect, even for the softest notes. I felt like I could have stayed entranced by the music forever, but soon the late hour bid us farewell to our guests. Invitations were extended to everyone for future visits and dinners, which saw many of our new friends at our house in the following weeks.

"A Dhow for the Day" or *"Sailing in the Sun"* All along the coast of Kenya, one could always see sailboats built in the same design as the old Arabian ships of the 17th century. They were called "Dhows", and their construction and materials, mostly wood and canvas, were the same as those of the 17th century.

"Dhows" in Lamu harbor

They ranged in size from small 15-foot-long fishing boats to large ocean-going ships of 60 feet in length that transported goods to the Arabian Peninsula and beyond to India. Their most distinctive feature was one large triangular canvas sail mounted on a long wooden beam that could be shifted from one side of the mast to the other, depending on the direction of the wind. We received several "invitations" from local fishermen to join them for a day of fishing.

So, one nice sunny day, we arranged to go sailing on a small dhow with a local fisherman named Mohammed. (I soon came to the conclusion that every third man in the Arab world must be named Mohammed!) Three other fellow travelers joined us, and along with four crew members, we sailed across the bay to a spot where the tide was low and the fishing promising.

A day of fishing on a Dhow - Lamu Island

There was a light wind in the morning as we slowly sailed up a small inlet to do some "goggling", while the crew stretched out a large net and slowly walked through the water to draw the net in a small circle to close the trap. Although some of the fish escaped because the net was for night fishing, not really suited to fishing in the middle of the day, they managed to catch some small fish and a stingray.

Meanwhile, as we were anchored next to a beautiful coral reef, a few in our group put on the goggles and dived into the water. The rest of us had little or no experience with snorkels and goggles, so we struggled with the gear. Having to wear eyeglasses, I was at a serious disadvantage, since they kept letting water leak into the mask, obscuring my vision. But I did manage to swim amongst the coral and see a few of the gorgeous tropical fish. John and Ginny were much better with the gear and spent much more time exploring the coral reef. For me it was a new and interesting experience, despite the handicap of the eyeglasses. As the fishermen labored in search of fish, we spent the time swimming in the bay and sunning on the deck. By the time the fish had been caught, the sun had become quite hot, so we pulled up anchor and sailed out of the bay toward the open ocean. As we reached the ocean, the small boat began to toss and pitch among the huge waves—a very thrilling ride to say the least! Then early in the afternoon, we hauled up on to the beach and cooked the fish and stingray over an open fire. The fishermen simply cleaned the fish and tossed them on to the hot coals. It was a primitive cooking method, but the results were excellent, especially with fresh squeezed lemon juice! It was my first taste of stingray and it was delicious—being light, firm meat arranged in parallel rows, with a delicate taste and just the hint of charcoal. As we enjoyed the fresh fish under the shade of some tall shrubs, we knew we had made a great choice to spend the day "fishing".

Following our leisurely lunch on the beach, we sailed back around the eastern side of the island, past the village of Shella and toward Lamu town. As the boat rounded the tip of the island, the wind suddenly picked up and the tide was near its highest point. The combination made for some really nice sailing, with some of the waves crashing over the bow and side of the boat, as the main sail billowed out to catch the full force of the wind. I felt I could have sailed like that all day. But alas, evening was fast approaching as we neared our house. We stepped off the boat into the shallow water, and as we walked up the beach to our house, I felt the quiet satisfaction of having "played" with nature—sailing in harmony with the raw elements of wind and sea. One would have to be blind and deaf not to feel the beauty of the day. That evening, we had a light dinner on the veranda, followed by coffee and quiet conversation under the light of the moon. Later, Marion and I massaged each other with scented oil to soothe the effects of the day's intense sun. It was the perfect ending to a beautiful day on the ocean!

"Marion and Mango Mania" Lamu Island was famous for its native fruit, the mango, a lovely yellow/ orange oval shaped fruit with a delicate tropical flavor and firm, juicy texture. It grew in such abundance on the island that it was very cheap to buy in the market. We bought a few mangos when we first arrived and continued buying more and more as time went on—they became a staple item in our diet. In fact, every time

one of us went into town to shop, mangos were always on the list. We ate them at breakfast, lunch, and dinner. The one person who always consumed the most mangos, and at the strangest hours, was Marion. John had his chocolate, Ginny had her milk and honey, I had my cold beer, and Marion had her mangos! We soon got used to seeing Marion with her mangos almost any time of day or night. Sometimes, she would have to eat a mango first thing in the morning, much the same as someone reaching for a smoke. I believe if we had kept count of her total mango consumption, it would have warranted a place in the Guinness Book of World Records! In spite of her "mango mania", we all loved her anyway.

"The Art of Cleaning Fish" On more than one occasion, one of the local fishermen would bring us a huge Rock Cod or Sea Bass. After a bit of bargaining to bring the price down to half of the initial price, I set about the task of cleaning and filleting the fish.

Marion with local fishermen and their catch of lobsters – Lamu Island

The first job was to gut the fish, which often weighed 20 pounds or more. The operation was done behind the house where it would not make a big mess. Once the fish was gutted, I had to filet it using one of the incredibly dull knives from our kitchen. I even tried, in vain, to sharpen the knives on the cement sidewalk, with little noticeable effect. But I managed to accomplish the task, despite the archaic cutting instruments. During our time on the island, I did all the cleaning of fish and boiling of crab and lobster, with the exception of one time when Marion bravely tackled the job. She did a marvelous job of it, even though it was pretty obvious she didn't enjoy it. The fish were always so large that the filet of one side would feed the four of us for two or three days. We used almost every part of the fish, making fish chowder with the leftover scraps of meat and bones. There were times when all the space in our freezer was taken up by fish.

The experience of cleaning fish was valuable, as well as being a necessary part of enjoying the bounty of the sea at mealtime. I also took on the job of boiling and cracking the crabs and lobsters. It was my first experience of boiling them alive, and I was a bit apprehensive in the beginning. A couple of times, the crabs were too large for the pot of boiling water, so

I either had to break off the claws first, which was quite tricky when the crabs were very active, or pour boiling water on them to stun them. But I quickly became adept at handling live crab and lobster—and in the end, the taste was well worth the effort.

"Last Day on Lamu Island" We had been living in paradise for nearly a month, but eventually, Ginny and Marion had to return home to family in Vancouver and London. We all knew that our time together on the island would not last forever, but the realization of our last day was still not something we looked forward to. That day on the island began the same as many others had before, very early with the sunrise, but with a note of sadness in the air. We had settled into a very peaceful, relaxed way of life and had grown to know the place so well. As we went about the day's activities, we knew it would be for the last time. There was our last shopping trip into town for a few small items needed to complete the menu for our final dinner party that evening. And there was the need to buy bus tickets for the return trip to Mombasa the following day. After which, we met up with Ray for coffee at Petley's Inn. Then we made a brief visit to the busy waterfront, before heading back to the house along a very familiar route.

Fisherman repairing net - Lamu town

We walked past the power generating station, the offices of the Ministry of Fish and Wildlife, and the Lamu Ginners factory. Marion and I spent the afternoon lying on the beach with Ray, and then we took a hike into the dunes behind "Peponi's Hotel" in Shella. After that, we went back to Peponi's for an icy cold fresh lemonade with Ray, before heading back to the house. Marion and I showered together and then massaged each other with lovely scented oil, while we listened to music and the sound of the wind in the palm trees outside our bedroom window. It was a moment that we both wished would last forever!

Just before dinner, as the sun was setting behind the dunes, Marion and I took a walk into the dunes to take some pictures. It was such a lovely warm evening that we ended up going all the way to the beach on the other side of the island. When we reached the beach, a heavy surf was rolling in, and as we walked along the sand, the waves played tag with our toes. Neither of us said very much, preferring to enjoy the evening on the beach, alone with our thoughts. As the night fell upon us, we headed back to the house to join our friends Ray and Seth for dinner on the veranda. Then we prepared dinner, which included anything and everything that was left over from the past month. In our customary style, we sat down to dinner by candlelight, followed by coffee and music on the veranda. It wasn't long before we were treated to a special event— the rising of the full moon. It began as a soft glow on the horizon, then the edge of a large orange ball peeked out over the top of the palm trees.

Slowly, it became larger and larger as it climbed into the dark night sky. As it rose higher, it began to change color, from deep orange to soft yellow, and finally brilliant white, beautifully reflected in the ripples of water of the bay. All of us sat silently on the veranda, spellbound by the glow of the moon. Just then, a large dhow quietly sailed past, silhouetted against the still water and the moonlight. The scene was almost a fantasy, like a wonderful dream! It was as if Lamu Island had bid us farewell. At that moment, I reflected upon all the wonderful times we had shared together over the past month on the island. We sat on the veranda for a long time without saying much, but to bid farewell to Lamu, each in our own way. Silently, the night slipped away, the moon rose higher in the night sky, the wind gently swept past us, and we retired to bed, along with our last dream of Lamu.

February 4, 1975
Lamu Island - Mombasa

"The Long Ride Back" The morning of our departure began early, as usual, with the rising of the sun. We had a quick breakfast and coffee on the veranda for the last time, before setting out on our final walk into town.

Marion and me leaving Lamu Island

Several times, I stopped, turned around, and looked back fondly at the beautiful house which held so many of my best memories. Ray was there to meet us on the dock and say goodbye as we boarded the boat back to the mainland. Once again, boarding was the usual scene of chaos and confusion, as well as the boat being overloaded. Later, as we climbed aboard the bus for the long, dusty, rough ride back to Mombasa, Lamu Island was but a beautiful memory. Yet, at the same time, we all yearned to return someday. Quickly, we claimed four seats and mentally prepared ourselves for the long 8-hour journey.

A few miles inland from the coast, the landscape abruptly changed to very flat, dry scrubland—in sharp contrast to the lovely white sandy beaches and gently swaying palm trees on the coast. Unfortunately, it made for a very dull and boring trip visually. And being on rough dirt roads for much of the route precluded any reading. We were praying that we would not have to endure the torture of chants from the Holy Quran again. Allah must have heard us, because our prayers were granted, and the loudspeaker remained silent for the entire trip! By the time we came to Malindi, halfway to Mombasa, we were already sore, tired, and hot.

The bus stopped for 30 minutes in Malindi, where John was to leave us for a while to do some travelling on his own. So, we all walked across the street to the one and only bar in town and shared a last beer together. All too soon, the bus was ready to continue the journey to Mombasa. Ginny and Marion bid John a hasty, but fond farewell, and then the three of us boarded the bus again. On the way from Malindi to Mombasa, the bus became very hot and cramped, for what seemed like an eternity. At one point along the way, everyone had to get off the bus as it rolled onto a small ferry. As passengers, we all had to pull a rope on the side of the ferry to move it across the river to the other side.

When I went to get back on the bus, there were twice as many passengers as had been on the opposite side of the river! I wondered, "how could that be"? As a result, I ended up having to "stand" most of the rest of the way to Mombasa. And to make matters even worse, the bus kept picking up more people along the side of the road. In fact, it seemed as if we stopped every 2 or 3 miles, which made the long journey so hot and uncomfortable, we were all exhausted by the time we reached the city. Marion had a severe headache, and Ginny wasn't feeling much better either. So, we quickly abandoned any thoughts of continuing on to Nairobi that night. Instead, we took a room at our old Mombasa hangout, the Visitor's Inn.

By the time we reached the inn, I also had a splitting headache, and all of us just crashed on the bed for a couple of hours, in an attempt to recover from the "Long Ride". Later, I took a shower and joined Ginny for dinner at the Curry Bowl, while Marion remained in the room recovering from the effects of the bus trip. For dinner, Ginny and I shared a massive plate of steak, liver, sausage, ham, bacon, chips, salad, bread, butter, and coffee for just over 17 schillings each (about $1.90)—what a fantastic deal! As we left the restaurant, we picked up some rolls and chips for Marion. Back in our room, we reminisced about the time we had spent on Lamu Island, and we all agreed it had been a once in a lifetime experience! In the morning we would be headed back to Nairobi, and the last day in Kenya for Ginny and Marion. But they would be taking fond memories of Africa with them as they returned home.

February 5-6, 1975
Mombasa to Nairobi

"Return to Nairobi" We arose early in the morning, after a restless night due to the noise and heat of the city—something from which we had escaped so well on Lamu Island. After breakfast, we checked the schedule of the bus to Nairobi. Then I thought it might be good to check the cost of a private taxi instead. As soon as we found out the cost of the taxi was only 15 schillings (about $1.80) more than the bus, we opted for the taxi—a much faster and more comfortable trip. The taxi wasn't scheduled to leave until 11:00am, so we walked to the "Swiss Bakery" for pastries and on to the "Kenya Coffee House", for a leisurely start to our last day together in Mombasa. Then we walked back to the Visitor's Inn, picked up our bags, and piled into a new Peugeot station wagon for the trip to Nairobi. The car was very comfortable as it cruised down the highway at 130 KPH, a speed I hadn't experienced since leaving the States 6 months before. It felt like we were in a racing car.

Along the way, we stopped to watch a large herd of elephants in Tsavo National Park, and caught a glimpse of Mt Kilimanjaro, before rolling into Nairobi and our usual hotel, the Hill Station Lodge. While Ginny went up to the Post Office to collect our mail, Marion and I checked into our old room, number 3. There was a message waiting for us from Krem, to say he wouldn't be able to see the girls off on their flight back home, as he had just taken a job at a mine south of Nairobi.

Ten minutes later, there was a knock on the door. As we opened it, there stood Scottish John! He had stopped by on the "off chance" we might be

163

back in town. We chatted for a few minutes about his latest adventures, and then we all walked up to our perennial meeting place, the New Stanley Hotel, for coffee with Ginny. After reading our mail over several cups of coffee, we went to the Iceland Milk Bar for dinner and their incredible fresh pineapple over crushed ice. Following dinner, we strolled around downtown and then decided to check out the cinema. The movie was titled "How to Ruin the Reputation of the World's Greatest Secret Agent", starring Jean Paul Belmondo and Jacqueline Bisset. Though it was a fairly predictable story line, we all enjoyed the film.

The next morning, after a rather restless night, caused by the anguished barking of the guard dog below our window, Marion and I went to SIAFU House to pick up stuff we had left behind while we were on Lamu Island. On the way, I stopped at the Post Office to pick up a package of film for my camera from my good friend Gordon in Seattle. I was very fortunate to get away with paying only 10 schillings duty on the shipment. But upon reaching SIAFU House, we found it vacant and deserted—the company had gone bankrupt! None of the neighbors knew where the SIAFU staff had moved our stuff, nor how to contact them. So, I left a note on the front door about how to contact us.

Then we headed to the New Avenue Hotel for lunch with Ginny, Scottish John, Canadian John and his wife Rabia. Along the way, Dave drove by in a SIAFU truck and told us he had given our stuff to Ginny. We chatted for a few minutes to catch up on his news, as the truck sat in the middle of the street. Apparently, our overland trip had cost the company so much money for the mechanical repairs and travel expenses beyond their initial budget, that the owner had no other option but to close down operations and declare bankruptcy. It was sad to hear, but not entirely unexpected. We bid farewell to Dave and continued on to the New Avenue Hotel.

After a lunch of enormous portions of delicious salads, and very enjoyable conversation with our friends, we hauled our gear back to our room. When the girls unpacked their bags, they had a real shock— someone had stolen most of their clothes they had left behind with the SIAFU staff! It was a real heartbreak for them, as many of their things were irreplaceable and of sentimental value. The experience turned the rest of the day sour and with a bad taste for Nairobi. So, that evening, I invited them for dinner at our favorite restaurant, the Bamboo Shoot. We shared a fantastic dinner of Chinese, Indonesian, and Indian food, as well as a lovely evening of intimate conversation—reflecting on our times together travelling in Africa! In some small measure, I hoped the evening would make up for the bad things that happened earlier in the day. After dinner, we walked slowly back to our room and the realization tomorrow would be our last day together in Africa. That night, Marion and I fell asleep in each other's arms!

February 7, 1975
Nairobi, Kenya

"Leaving on a Jet Plane" or *"Farewell my Love"* It was a night where none of us got much sleep, as a result of the anticipation of what was to come with the arrival of daylight. We awoke early, and after breakfast we made preparations to take the baggage, what was left of it, to the East African Airways Terminal downtown. From there, we boarded the shuttle bus to the airport, and when we arrived, to our dismay, we found a very long line of people waiting to check in for the charter flight to London. Some were loaded down with everything but the kitchen sink! Woefully, we joined the ranks to wait our turn with the inevitable red tape of immigration and customs procedures. Aware of the situation, Ginny graciously volunteered to remain in the queue with the bags to allow Marion and I to make the most of our last few moments together. As we walked arm in arm around the small terminal building, there wasn't much either of us could say to ease the sadness and pain of the moment. Ironically, even when we tried to share some coffee at a small kiosk, their coffee maker was broken! All too soon, the time came for flight check-in, and amidst the rush of shuffling bags and rustling paperwork, we were lost in the mechanism of departure.

Suddenly, the only step left was through Immigration and Customs, where I couldn't follow. At that moment, the realization fell upon us like a crescendo of falling water. I had but a brief moment in time to say goodbye to someone I deeply yearned to hold forever! As we hugged each other until our ribs ached, I felt all my deepest and most solitary emotions swell up inside me and burst forth as a pool of moisture in my eyes. And after a final brief but impassioned kiss, I blurted out "goodbye" and wished her a safe journey home. I held her hand as long as it was physically possible, until I was forced to let go and turn away.

As I walked haltingly toward the observation deck, in the hope of having a fleeting glimpse of her as she boarded the plane, I dared not look back, for her tears would have been too much for me to bear gracefully. I climbed the stairs steadily, but in no rush, for I knew it would be at least a half hour before the departure of the flight. Meanwhile, I attempted to buy some coffee at the snack bar, but as I stood in line, I became terribly self-conscious of my watery, blood-shot eyes and the forlorn look on my face. So, I quickly walked over to the chain link fence to watch the plane, a British Airways jet sitting alone on the edge of the airfield. For a long time, I was unaware of everything going on around me, even the intense heat of the sun beating incessantly on my head. I preferred to recount some of the most memorable moments we had shared.

Suddenly, I became aware of the shuttle vans that would take passengers from the waiting lounge to the plane. They began moving to the plane, but no matter how much I strained, I couldn't see the passengers as I had hoped. Anxiously, I watched the shuttle vans as they pulled up to the boarding door, one by one. My eyes strained in the bright sunshine, trying to search the line of passengers for the one I loved. They were all so far away, I thought I wouldn't have a hope of seeing her.

But, all of a sudden, I spotted a little figure in light blue jeans and jacket—I waved frantically, in the hope she would see me. I believe she did, for the tiny blue figure waved back, before disappearing into the huge jet. I began to think about how she might be feeling at the moment, settling into her seat as the plane prepared for takeoff. One by one, the service vehicles pulled away and the jet engines began to roar. The huge bulk slowly taxied down the runway, as I watched with tense muscles, almost motionless, with anticipation as it waited near the end of the runway for another plane to land. After a few minutes, it slowly turned its face to the north and lumbered down the runway, past the terminal building. Gradually and steadily it gained speed, and as it passed me, all the emotions of the past few hours burst forth, and my eyes could not hold them in any longer!

I kept watching, as best as I could through the wet windows of my heart, as the jet rose into the sky above me. She was on her way home to London, and I stood alone now in the brilliant sunshine of East Africa. After some ten minutes of staring blankly into the clear blue sky, I turned and went in search of coffee, in the hope of calming my tangled and spent emotions. I sipped the cup of coffee slowly as I watched another plane load its passengers. But I was not really focused on much beyond the emptiness of my soul! A half hour of waiting in the terminal, a ride aboard a busload of Japanese tourists, and I was back to Nairobi, where I wandered around a bit aimlessly, until the feeling of hunger grabbed my brain. I spent the afternoon sipping coffee and a beer in a number of familiar places, as I composed a letter to my lost love, now somewhere high above Africa. That evening I went to the cinema in a vain attempt to lose myself in the movie, but I came out feeling more alone than ever and facing a night in a familiar bed with all the emptiness of my heart. It felt so cold in the room that night, despite the warm air—a paradoxical feeling that seemed very real at the time. I was numbed by the experience of her leaving, and slowly the significance and impact reached my brain. Eventually, the long night became day, and I was still alone!

February 8, 1975
Nairobi to Mombasa

"Night Train from Nairobi" I awoke early, as usual, determined to occupy my mind with the details of travel plans, necessities to buy, and things to check on. There was a trip to the Sudan Embassy to enquire about a tourist visa and the current security situation in the country. In one word, I was told travel was NOT advised at the moment, due to terrorist activity in the south of the country. In addition, travel to Somalia wasn't recommended as well. So, the original idea that John and I had about travelling north to Egypt looked pretty bleak and out of the question. I busied myself browsing through bookstores and a visit to the Iceland

Milk Bar, which had suddenly become a different place for me. After coffee at the Thorn Tree Café, I headed to the bus station to check on tickets and schedule of buses to Mombasa, where John and I had arranged to meet up after Ginny and Marion had departed for London. When I got to the bus station, the line for tickets was incredibly long and slow moving, so I decided to check out the train instead.

I trundled off to the railway station, where I found another queue, but at least it was much shorter. First, I had to request a reservation on the 6:30pm train to Mombasa. Then from the reservations desk, I stepped across the lobby to the ticket window to buy one second class ticket. After which, I went back to the reservations desk to "confirm" my reservation. Finally, I shuttled back across the lobby to the ticket agent to get a booking for a seat and compartment assignment. It was a lengthy process, but certainly a foolproof system! Having received final instructions from the ticket agent, I headed back to the Thorn Tree Café for a cold beer, and spent the afternoon engaged in writing letters and postcards to family and friends.

Soon, it was time to pick up my bag at the Hill Station Lodge and head to the railway station. I arrived at the station to find the usual mass of confusion, so typical of my experience in Africa. I made my way through the crowd to board the train, having had a lot of experience riding trains in Europe. But I could see for the vast majority of the passengers, that it looked as if it was their first trip on a train.

Once on board, I settled into my compartment (car 2160, compartment D, and met my new traveling companions, two young English guys also going to Mombasa. One was all hyped up about railroads and talked incessantly about them, to the point of sheer boredom! (he soon became obnoxious His friend wasn't much better company, with his "beekeeping" stories, but at least he wasn't as talkative, although he kept encouraging his buddy to keep on "bullshitting" about virtually nothing of any substance or significance. (it was strictly a pure case of noise with no sense

Later, I managed to make a break from the oppressive atmosphere of the compartment by taking a reservation for dinner in the dining car. It was a beautiful old car in the most classic sense, with crisp white linen on heavy oak tables, fine English china, shiny silver flatware, soft leather upholstered chairs, and soft lights! The first call for dinner was announced by a steward ringing chimes in the passageway. As I entered the dining car, it looked as if it was straight out of the 1940's, like the New York Central Railroad's elegant and sophisticated "Broadway Limited" train. Over the next two hours, I enjoyed a 7-course affair of perfectly roasted beef, along with generous portions of sautéed fresh vegetables, Yorkshire pudding, potatoes, and fresh baked dinner rolls, all served graciously by stewards in black tie. I felt very comfortable and relaxed as I savored dinner, while the car gently swayed from side to side and clicked past the miles of rails in the warm night. (dinner was most certainly the highlight of my train journey) I finished the dinner experience with a glass of Drambuie, before returning to my compartment.

Much to my pleasure, I found everyone turning down the bunks and preparing for sleep, which was most agreeable with me. I settled into one of the top bunks as the lights were turned out, and promptly zoomed off into dreams of Marion. The car swayed gently to and fro along the steel rails into the darkness of the East African Plains. It was a blissful night until the train stopped somewhere in the middle of nowhere for an interminable amount of time. At that point, I was awakened by the sound of snoring, so loud it virtually rattled the windows and vibrated the floor! I found it impossible to sleep above the barrage of snoring, since there was no rail noise to drown it out. I even tried to discreetly wake the guy in the bunk below me, in hopes of ending his nasal contortions, but to no avail. Finally, I had no choice but to get up and walk around the train until it began to move again. When I returned to the compartment, I was able to slip into quiet slumber again, lulled by the rhythm of the rails and embraced by the dream of Marion in my arms.

Only one other time was I awakened by the "snore", and then just briefly, so the majority of the journey to Mombasa was pleasant—in stark comparison to the "Midnight Bus to Mombasa"! By sunrise, we were still far from Mombasa and obviously behind schedule—I couldn't understand why it would take 12–14 hours to travel from Nairobi to Mombasa, a distance of only 275 miles. However, I was on no particular timeline, so I wasn't really concerned. I took the opportunity to visit the dining car again for a delicious traditional full English breakfast.

While I enjoyed my breakfast, the train approached an unusual and unique engineering feature, a complete 360-degree loop designed to enable the train to descend the steep slope of the 2400-foot high Mashunda Escarpment, from the plateau down to the coast. As the sun rose higher in the morning sky, we finally began to approach Mombasa, past the busy waterfront, a large steel mill, railyard and into the station. As I had expected, the mass of passengers all headed for the one and only exit gate at the same time. I managed to survive the "stampede", together with the two English dudes who tagged along because I had made the stupid mistake of saying I had been to Mombasa before. The three of us walked out of the station and down Haile Selassie Avenue, where I showed them the bus station and a place to sleep, the Cozy Guest House. Then we went for a morning coffee at the Kenya Coffee House.

Finally, I asked them if they could manage on their own, since I needed to get down to Tradewinds Lodge on the south coast to meet up with John. Then I rushed to the bus station, just in time to find out that I had missed the one and only scheduled bus to Ukunda, the nearest town to Tradewinds Lodge. But I was informed that I could try one of the "country buses" that departed from across the street. So, I walked up to one of them and asked the driver of the dilapidated heap of metal and rubber, if he was going to Ukunda. Indeed, he was and would be leaving right away. Knowing the concept of time in Africa, I figured I most likely had time to run back to the Visitor's Inn, grab my gear, and return to the bus station. Upon returning, I discovered his bus had left, but that there was another equally dilapidated wreck waiting.

So, I boarded the old wreck, handed 5 schillings to the young man standing at the door, and proceeded to find a seat on the overcrowded old bus. Eventually, we departed Mombasa, after some passengers pushed the old bus to get it started. As we left the station, people were still jumping on and off the bus when we pulled on to Kenyatta Avenue and headed south. I began to develop a theory that the people who jumped off the bus just before departure, were acting as "decoys" to lure more passengers to board the bus in order to leave on time—country buses and taxis tended to wait until they had the number of passengers they deemed necessary to make money. It was a strategy I would encounter firsthand in my final days in Kenya. The old bus bumped and bounced down the highway amidst the heavy noon day traffic—the engine coughed and sputtered at times, and thick black diesel smoke belched from the rear, while the front end wandered all over the road. Still, the old girl kept chugging away! Once we had crossed the Kilindini River on the Likoni Ferry, which allowed large vessels passage to and from the port to the Indian Ocean, the bus began the frustrating practice of stopping for every Tom, Dick, and Harry standing anywhere near the side of the road. It became abundantly clear that the bus had no schedule or passenger limit! It was a mad scene of stopping every two or three miles to pick up or drop off people, until at last, my stop came up at a crossroads outside of Ukunda.

As we approached it, all I could see was a large sign for Tradewinds Lodge and a big red arrow pointing down a narrow dirt road. We made what would be loosely termed a "flying stop". As the bus approached the sign, a guy leaped aboard the top of the bus to retrieve my bag, and I was instructed to stand at the door. Then the guy on top of the bus tossed my bag to another guy standing on the edge of the road, and I was given the "go" signal as a tap on my shoulder. I jumped out the door as the guy who had caught my bag from the roof of the bus ran to catch up with it.

Then, the driver floored the throttle of the old beast and thick, black smoke poured out of the engine as the "baggage" man ran frantically alongside the bus, with one hand securely clinging to the handrail of the door. After 50 feet or so, he swung gracefully on to the bus and slapped the side of it loudly, as if to give the "all clear" signal to the driver, whose reaction seemed to indicate he could have cared less! As the old bus roared off down the highway, I was left standing alone in the hot sun alongside the road to Tradewinds Lodge and my rendezvous with John.

February 9, 1975
Mombasa – Twiga Beach

"The Magic Snake" I began walking down the dirt road with my backpack, which had become heavier, now that I was carrying all my worldly possessions in it. As I was hoping for a ride to come along, two cars of wealthy white tourists passed me as if I was just another telephone pole beside the road! Then nothing came along for what seemed like several hours in the hot sun. As I continued to hike down the lonely road, I thought to myself, "this will get me in shape to climb Kilimanjaro"! After another couple of hours and 5 miles later, a little "jeep-like" thing came along, with a heavy-set white guy driving and a tall black man hanging on the side of the vehicle.

All of a sudden, they screeched to a halt and asked where I was headed. When I replied, "Tradewinds Lodge", they bid me to hop in the back. I sat on my backpack among several bags and a couple of large covered baskets, as we roared down the rough dirt road. I made an attempt at a bit of polite conversation, but the heavy-set guy spoke very little English, mostly German. And the black guy kept acting as someone really "cool", but nothing of what he said was halfway intelligible or made any sense. As we neared Tradewinds Lodge, the "cool" black dude began saying something about a "magic snake" and tapping the German guy on the top of his head! So, I just smiled and nodded as he continued his "magic snake" bit.

Finally, we approached the parking lot and the heavy-set guy, being half drunk, promptly went the wrong way. That was when I said, "this is just fine, I'll get out here", but they wouldn't hear of it, unfortunately. The big guy stopped, shoved the jeep into reverse, and promptly backed into a large tree. It shook the hell out of me and bent the fender up against the rear wheel! Undeterred, he put it into forward gear and zoomed off in the right direction, the rear tire smoking like mad! But it was of no concern to these guys. At last, we screeched to a stop in the parking lot and I was able to extricate myself from the "mad machine". But, as I pulled my backpack out of the back of the vehicle, the black dude pulled a huge snake out of one of the covered baskets, right in front of my nose, and uttered the familiar words "magic snake"! Then he proceeded to wrap it around his neck. By that time, John had come up from the pool with an English family he had met earlier, and they all got into the act, taking photos of the black dude and his "magic snake". As to what was the "magic", I had no real clue, but it had definitely been a wild ride and a "flashy" arrival at Tradewinds Lodge.

Later that afternoon, I joined John for sandwiches and beer at the bar, a swim in the pool, and a reunion with Joe, who was there with his new overland group awaiting visas to enter the Sudan. Then at 4:00pm sharp, we joined the English family for tea and crumpets poolside. Following the customary afternoon tea, John and I walked down the beach to "Twiga Lodge", which was to be our place of residence on the south coast of Kenya for perhaps a week or more. That evening, as we sat in the lounge, awaiting the time for dinner, John flashed the news on me about a ship to India leaving Mombasa in 10 days—would I consider going to India with him?

Well, his news hit me rather unexpectedly and at an awkward moment. So, I sat silently while John went through his rationale—Mozambique was a little too farfetched for tourists now, the situation in Ethiopia and Somalia was nothing short of "tough going", and besides, Africa was becoming a bit boring for him. After a nice dinner and some thought, I said "I'll consider it, but I've always counted on climbing Kilimanjaro before leaving Africa". That was when John introduced me to a group of overland travelers he had met on the beach the day before, one of whom was Liam who had gone fishing with us on Lamu Island. They would be leaving for Tanzania in the morning, so I made a quick decision to join them. John and I agreed to meet up at Twiga Lodge when I returned from Kilimanjaro, and at that point I would let him know one way or the other if I would join him on the ship to India. That night, we rolled out our sleeping bags on the beach and were lulled to sleep by the gentle sound of the surf and the soft breeze in the palm trees above us.

Twiga beach south of Mombasa, Kenya

CHAPTER EIGHT

February 10, 1975
Twiga Beach - Mombasa - Marangu, Tanzania

"*Meeting with Mt. Kilimanjaro*" or "*What about India*" The rising sun woke me early on the beach, and I spent some time wandering along its broad expanse, lined with swaying palm trees. Then I joined John in the lounge for toast and coffee, before we met up with Liam and his group for the trip into Mombasa. We roared down the highway in Liam's old red Land Rover to the tunes of Bob Dylan and the Rolling Stones blasting at full volume from the speakers. That was when I knew I would be in for quite a trip over the next week or 10 days. Liam and company went to get visas at the Tanzanian embassy, while John and I checked on the boat to India. Our first stop was the Indian embassy, where we were told there wasn't enough time to get visas, but that we really didn't need them anyway? Next was a visit to the travel agency to check on the details of the sailing to Bombay. After some lengthy and tedious calculations, it was determined that we would need to make a deposit of 400 schillings to reserve space on board and pay the balance of the one way fare within two weeks of the sailing—but since the ship was scheduled to sail in 10 days, what exactly was required, the deposit or the full fare? They didn't know, and besides, it was now noon and the office was closing for lunch.

By that time, Liam was getting ready to leave for Tanzania and John was anxious to get a ticket for the ship. And as for me, I had to make a quick decision. If I decided at that point to go to India with John, I would have to cash some travelers checks before the banks closed. At the same time, I asked myself, "did I really want to go to India"? And, "would I be able to get a refund of the ticket if I later decided not to go"? It was all just too much hassle in too short of time, so I said "John, I'm not going to India today or in 10 days from now, maybe some other time"! I could see by his expression he was disappointed and sad, since I think he had counted on me saying yes. Then his sadness turned into indecision about his own plans. Finally, we put the whole thing on hold and went to the Kenya Coffee House to meet up with Liam. There we found him wolfing down an iced coffee with ice cream. Over a cup of delicious Kenyan coffee, I told John I would meet up with him in 10 days, in Mombasa either the day the boat was scheduled to sail, or he would leave me a note at the Post office if his plans changed. Then I bid him farewell, joined the Kilimanjaro group as they piled into the Land Rover, and roared off down the road to Tanzania. As we left Mombasa behind us, I couldn't help wondering if I had made the right decision.

It was a beautiful trip to the border as we passed lots of ostriches and elephants in Tsavo National Park. I broke out my small collection of cassette tapes, and soon found out my selection of music was a welcome change from the tunes they had been listening to for such a long time. As the sounds of David Crosby, Santana, and Roberta Flack floated into my ears, my thoughts went back to the days on Lamu Island. Fond, misty memories filled my head and I seemed to be floating in my own world as I lay among the bags in the back, swaying and rocking with the Land Rover as it roared down the rough gravel road—it felt almost like a daydream.

We crossed the border into Tanzania with no problem, and an hour later, as evening approached, we came to the "Marangu Hotel". In the dim light of sunset, we had a glimpse of the mountain, its summit shrouded in a fluffy blanket of pink clouds that spilled over the side of the peak and cascaded down the slope like a giant waterfall. We were told about a small campsite behind the hotel by a group of German and Austrian climbers. So, we set up camp and then went to the hotel office to check-in. We were promptly "chewed out" by a prim old lady for not having reported to the office first. We were apparent victims of inadequate signage or notices. The experience was a foretaste of future hassles with the Marangu Hotel management. After dinner and a couple of beers in the hotel lounge, we retired to our campsite in the cool, crisp mountain air.

February 11-12, 1975
Marangu, Tanzania

"Waiting for the Mountain" We awoke to a pleasantly cool day under the shade of the huge trees in the hotel garden, where we were camped, as we waited for space to open up in the mountain huts. Confirmed reservations for space in the huts was required to obtain permits to climb the mountain, which was managed by the National Park Service of Tanzania. We spent the day lounging in the old hotel, a series of rooms surrounding a lovely courtyard full of beautiful red and gold flowers. The lounge and dining room were filled with old wooden and leather furnishings, nothing pretentious, just warm and homey. Surrounding the old hotel were several small gardens, huge old trees, spacious lawns, and an area of pens and hutches for everything from chickens and rabbits to ducks and goats. Another resident of the "Marangu Menagerie" was a "bush baby", a small, shy, retiring creature native to the tropical forest. We usually began our day with a hearty breakfast in the dining room and took dinner every evening in the hotel as well. Meals were always solid, hearty home cooked German food, but it was served by a sour, grumpy, capricious staff who often went out of their way to let us know it was a real "pain in the ass" to serve us! Fortunately, it never took anything away from our enjoyment of the delicious food.

I often spent the afternoons relaxing in the warm sunshine, writing in my journal, and reading Rachel Carson's book, "The Edge of the Sea". (it was ironic, since we were over a hundred eighty miles from the ocean) Early in the mornings, just after sunrise, and early in the evenings, the summit of Mt Kilimanjaro was visible from the hotel garden.

Mt Kilimanjaro from Marangu Hotel campground

It was a very imposing sight, almost like it was directly above us—the view was more than enough to inspire us for the climb to the top! After dinner in the evenings, we would usually sit in the lounge, share a few beers with the German and Austrian climbers, and talk about our "date" with the mountain. Then we would all head to the campsite and retire for the night under the stars. I always rolled out my sleeping bag under a picnic table so as to avoid the heavy dew that showed up every morning. I reserved my nights for quiet dreams of my love in London—they were always something I looked forward to. But they were all too short, broken by the first light of the rising sun in the morning.

February 13, 1975
Marangu, Tanzanzia

"Monsoon in Marangu" This day was pretty much the same as the past two days, except that everyone but me drove into Moshi, the nearest large town, to buy some provisions and attempt to change money on the black market. I spent the day relaxing beneath the huge trees overlooking the garden, writing in my journal and reading Rachel Carson's book. Later in the afternoon, the group returned with lots of fruit and a rate of 13

schillings to the dollar, almost double the official exchange rate at the bank! We were happy about the success with changing money, but also a bit apprehensive because the hotel was not supposed to accept any money without official bank exchange receipts. As it turned out, they never required us to show the official exchange receipts, although they were empowered to do so. That evening, we all enjoyed a wonderful dinner of traditional German schnitzel and potato salad. Then we took our after-dinner coffee sitting in the lounge around a roaring fire in the old stone fireplace. Suddenly, the wind picked up speed, the windows began to rattle, and the bushes in the garden shook—a clear sign of an impending storm. Within a few minutes, the deluge of rain began—first as a soft patter of raindrops on the roof, followed by light drumming on the slate roof shingles as the raindrops united.

Finally, the rain turned into "waves" of water beating with incredible force on the roof above us. I couldn't stand the tension any longer and felt compelled to witness the event first-hand. As I stood in the open doorway, feeling the brisk wind in my face, I watched as wave after wave of heavy rain crashed against the buildings, flowers, bushes and garden. The ground quickly became a small river and soon a lake, as water poured off the hotel roof in steady streams. At one point, I feared the roof might not be able to with-stand the torrent of water and the incessant pounding of the rain. On and on it continued, for more than an hour, never letting up its fury! Then, all of a sudden, the onslaught of the storm ended as quickly as it had begun, and gently faded away into the night. The raging waters subsided, the land appeared again, and the evening air was refreshed as if it was the coming of spring! It was an incredible phenomenon of nature I would remember for a long time after. Not trusting the night to remain clear, we rolled out our sleeping bags under the shelter of a small hut, to await yet another day in the shadow of Mt Kilimanjaro.

February 14, 1975
Marangu, Tanzania

"An Afternoon by the Waterfall" The day began with word that we would be permitted to start our climb of Mt Kilimanjaro the following day. We were all excited with the news and made final arrangements with the Kibo Hotel for a guide, porters, and gear that was required for the 5-day climb. After we confirmed the permits, paid the fees, and met our climbing guide, we decided to visit a lovely waterfall about two miles upstream from the hotel. As we hiked up the road, always with Kilimanjaro in our sight, we had visions of what the climb to the summit might be like. A narrow trail to the waterfall led us through the dense forest and past some banana plantations. Soon, we came to a cool, clear mountain stream, bubbling over huge boulders into small pools of water shining in the bright sun. Along the trail, I spotted a small pool that looked especially inviting and secluded. So, I decided to stop there, while the rest of the group hiked up the trail to the waterfall. The pool was hidden by a steep slope and surrounded by thick forest. I climbed down to the edge of the pool and tested it "gingerly" with my toes. The crystal-clear water was cold, but not unpleasantly so. I quietly slipped out of my clothes and waded into the icy water, until I stood up to my knees.

Then I "plunged" in and found it to be very invigorating and refreshing! I splashed and paddled around in the water, enjoying the beautiful "seclusion" of my private pool! After an hour or so of invigoration in the cold stream, I climbed out on to a sun swept rock to relax and bathe in the warm rays of the sun as it dried my nude body with intense warmth. Later, I took another short dip in the pool and then retired to a comfortable spot on a large rock beside the mountain stream. As the water tumbled over the huge boulders, it provided a constant musical interlude as I did some writing in my journal. At least two or three hours passed as quickly as minutes in a day. Then I decided to join my friends at the waterfall, and as I approached, I saw it plunged more than 50 feet into a large pool.

Waterfall near Marangu Hotel, Tanzania

Everyone in the group was stretched out on the lush grass beside the pool. It was an idyllic scene, reminiscent of an old-world painting of people reclined under large trees beside a stream. It was like a piece of art I had seen in the Tate Museum of London. We all lay on the grass until the sun's rays failed to reach us any longer—then we bid farewell to the beautiful secluded spot and headed back to the hotel to prepare ourselves for the climb to the summit of Mt Kilimanjaro in the morning.

February 15-19, 1975
Marangu, Tanzania

"Kilimanjaro—An Experience of the Highest"

[**Day 1**] I began the day with a cold shower at 6:00am and breakfast at 7:00am, before we all gathered our gear and met up with our guide and porters, in preparation for the 5-day expedition to the summit of Mt Kilimanjaro. As we were about to depart, Petra had a run-in with the hotel owner for having entered the kitchen to boil some eggs without first obtaining permission. It was a clear case of not respecting the "chain of command", and she received a harsh reprimand from the hotel owner. When we prepared to leave the hotel and begin our trek up the trail, the owner, a little "beady-eyed" man with a Hitler style mustache, gave us final instructions in a stern voice and bid us a safe journey. At that point, I almost felt obligated to "salute"! The first three miles of the route followed a new gravel road up to the Kilimanjaro National Park entrance gate. Our guide and porters insisted that before we left civilization behind, we had to make a stop for banana beer, known locally as "Bombay Bomb"! The taste was rather bitter and heavily fermented— it stretched the traditional definition of "beer". But we all shared a cup with the crew before entering the national park.

Once inside the park, the trail quickly became more primitive, but relatively free of rocks and a steady uphill grade. It felt so lovely and free to be hiking through the lush forest without the oppressive burden of a 40-pound pack on my back. Following the slow steady pace of the porters gave me time to fully appreciate the surrounding countryside, a beautiful combination of coniferous forest and equatorial woodland. The weather of the day was perfect, with clear blue skies and pleasantly warm temperatures. Earlier in the day, as we had prepared to leave our campsite at the hotel, the view of Mt Kilimanjaro was spectacular and beckoned us upward. Around mid-day we stopped for lunch beside a small stream, and the crystal clear, cold spring water afforded my feet a welcome dip. We also met several people along the trail on their way down from the mountain, and they told us stories of how tough the climb was—not something we wanted to hear just then. But we would be undaunted from our goal of reaching the summit. After hiking another couple of hours, we were in sight of Mandara Hut (#1) at 9,000 feet elevation. Just below the hut, the trail entered a large open field that afforded us a fantastic view of the hills and vast East African plains far below. We could even see Lake Manyara and the town of Arusha in the distance, over 100 miles away.

As we got close to the hut, the landscape changed abruptly to meadows of thick grassland, intermingled with juniper shrubs and small coniferous forest along the nearby stream. The hut was nothing fancy, but it was comfortable, with bunks, a large table, and an old stone fireplace. There were two other climbing parties on their way down, so a lot of people were lounging around the hut, sharing their experiences of reaching the summit. As I stood on the front porch of the hut, I had an amazing 180-degree panoramic view of the entire northeast corner of Tanzania— it was such an awe-inspiring sight, that I wondered what awaited me on the summit! Precisely at 4:00pm, we were served hot tea and biscuits, a continuation of the old British influence. As we sat on the lush green grass outside the hut, with the vast expanse of the East African plains below us, we listened to the mellow sound of Santana on my cassette tape player—a beautiful moment to remember!

View of Tanzania from Mandara hut

While the sun slowly descended behind the mountain and evening fell upon us, the porters served us a delicious dinner of vegetable soup, Swiss steak, boiled potatoes, carrots, fresh fruit and coffee. From our table beside the fireplace, we looked out upon a beautiful, multi-hued landscape of orange and red that slowly transformed into deeper, more somber shades, eventually becoming a single color—black.

Soon, we became aware of the chilly night air and the blanket of a billion stars overhead. It was a spectacular light show for our benefit. Far below us, the lights of many small towns and villages twinkled in the night. Off in the distance, we could see a few spots of orange glow from a huge brush fire far to the south. The rest of the evening was spent playing cards by the light of a kerosene lantern and a roaring fire in the stone fireplace. About 8:30pm, everyone's eyelids became so heavy that we all headed for our bunks and bid each other pleasant dreams—knowing the morning would arrive early and the start of day two.

[**Day 2**] We were awakened before dawn by our guide who brought us cups of hot tea to take off the chill of the night and give some light to our eyes. As I sipped the hot tea, still huddled in my warm sleeping bag, the first rays of sunshine began to give color and life to the landscape outside the hut. Slowly, as we awakened to the day, so did Mt Kilimanjaro. As I climbed out of my sleeping bag, I stumbled around trying to find my boots and my camera to capture the spectacular sunrise. I stood on the front porch of the hut and took several pictures of the vast sea of clouds below us, as the sun painted them with soft, golden shades of orange,pink, and red. At last, a fiery ball peeked over the eastern hills and announced the official beginning of the day. It was not long after sunrise that our porters served us a hearty breakfast of fresh mango, bananas, hot porridge and boiled eggs. Soon it was time to pack up our gear and prepare to move out. We left the hut around 7:30am, with our porters in the lead. But we soon outdistanced them, as they were carrying heavy loads at a much slower pace up the steep trail. As I watched them, most being smaller than me, I was very impressed by their incredible agility and stamina, especially since they were so ill-equipped compared to us. Many wore old, worn out "plastic" shoes, while others had no socks and just old ragged sandals.

The first mile of the trail descended through thick forest covered in moss and lichens hanging from the trees. It was a lovely scene with the early morning light softly filtered through the dense canopy—it gave us the feeling of being back in the tropical jungle, except for the effect of the chilly morning air. Then, all of a sudden, the trail left the edge of the dense forest and emerged into a huge open grassy meadow, with a beautiful view of the snowcapped summit of Kilimanjaro.

On the trail to Horumbo Hut

As we tread lightly through the lush grass, there remained a bit of frost covering the ground. From that point, the trail crossed mostly open grassland, sagebrush, and a low growing form of juniper. The trail itself was in good condition, with only a few large rocks along the way. It climbed at a slow, steady grade over several low ridges. As we neared an elevation of 11,000 feet, the trail crossed through some rocky canyons with small streams and a strange palm-like plant with a top in the shape of a burning candle. The scene resembled a scattering of birthday candles spread atop a rocky cake! I even imagined a light snowfall would make the scene look like "icing" on the cake—a very bizarre and fascinating illusion! Just beyond the "birthday candles", the trail passed above a huge wildfire burning in the juniper brush on the steep slope below. The thick smoke obscured our view to the south. I remembered having seen a small spot of smoke high on the southern face of the mountain from the Marangu Hotel campsite two days before. At the time, I thought it might have been caused by the thunderstorm the day before.

Early in the afternoon, after hiking 12 miles of trail, we arrived at Horumbo Hut (#2 in time for lunch. At an elevation of 12,000 feet, we were starting to feel some effects of the high altitude, though I still felt strong and in good shape—confident I would be able to reach the summit.

After lunch, I sat outside the hut reading my book, and I noticed some curious little mouse-like creatures scurrying around gathering dry grass. Soon it was time for an early dinner of roasted chicken, rice, potatoes, carrots and soup. A large party of Swiss climbers had just come down from the summit, so there were a shortage of bunks and a few people had to double up for the night. Following dinner, I walked out to a point of rock where there was a spectacular view of the sunset as it painted the mountain and clouds in a beautiful spectrum of orange and red. As I watched the sunset, I could see the glow of the brush fire that had been burning for the past three days. Later in the evening, we were told by one of the guides it been started by a campfire and two porters were jailed for having started it. The fire had spread rapidly over a large area below Horumbo hut, and apparently it had already crossed over the trail below, forcing some hikers to scurry around it. That night, an older Swiss gentleman played a few folk tunes on his harmonica before lanterns were turned out and we all headed for bed. We tried to get some sleep, but it became difficult at times.

Horumbo hut – start of day 3

[**Day 3**] We arose early as usual, before dawn, and heard a howling wind blowing outside—just the sound of it made us feel a lot colder. Once again, our guide brought us hot tea to get our blood flowing, so we could manage to hop out of our warm bunks. Then he advised us it would be a day we could expect to really feel the effects of the high altitude. Already I had begun to notice heavy breathing and pounding heartbeat, even while I was at rest. After another hearty breakfast, we slowly made our way up the trail again. Our guide continued to emphasize the importance of going slowly to avoid exhaustion, so we followed the pace of the porters ahead of us. It was a very steady, comfortable pace up the steep slope toward a long ridge between the base of Kilimanjaro and its little sister to the east, Mawenzi Peak. After four miles up the steep grade, the trail reached the crest of the ridge. From that point, the trail stretched out another five miles across the broad, rocky saddle that resembled a barren desert—but bitterly cold.

On the trail to Kibo hut

The strong wind drove the cold air through our skin like sharp nails—not what one would imagine as Africa! As long as we kept moving, it wasn't too bad, but as soon as we stopped, even for a brief moment, the cold went deep into our bones. It was no exaggeration to say that we weren't really prepared for such a drastic change in the climate. It felt more like the North Pole than the Equator! The final two miles to reach Kibo Hut (#3) became a very steep, heartbreaking trek, as the hut looked so close yet so far away. The last 300 yards were very difficult, due to the steepness of the trail and the high altitude. We finally arrived at Kibo hut about 1:00pm in the afternoon and quickly arranged our gear in the hut.

That afternoon, all of us experienced the effect of the thin air as we attempted to catch some sleep at 15,500 feet elevation. But due to the lack of breath and bad headaches, it was nearly impossible. Later, a few people became nauseous, a common malady of "mountain sickness". I couldn't eat anything that evening and had to take four aspirin for my headache. One of the German guys gave me one of his sleeping pills, and I managed to fall asleep for a couple of hours, until we were awakened at midnight by our guide with cups of hot tea and biscuits.

[**Day 4**] We drank our hot tea and I managed to eat a couple of biscuits before we got dressed for the final assault to the summit. It was literally a matter of putting on every available piece of clothing, including two pair of pants, to brave the subzero cold of the night. It was a real shock to hop out of a warm sleeping bag, but after a few minutes, I felt in pretty good shape compared to earlier that night. However, there were many who didn't feel quite so fit. As we stumbled out of the hut, it was pitch black, bitterly cold, and the wind was whistling like a mad hawk! At 1:00am, we began to follow our guide up the steep, sandy trail, hardly able to see one foot in front of the other so we just followed the shadowy figure ahead. I had nothing to break the strong bitter cold wind as it stung my face in the dark. With our walking sticks, we steadied ourselves in the soft volcanic ash and probed for large rocks in our path. At one point, my eyeglasses became so fogged up that I felt like a blind man swinging his cane in all directions, desperately trying to find his way. The "trail" was hardly a trail at all, and it was very frustrating to make any headway in the soft volcanic ash. It was a matter of zigzagging across the steep slope, and for every step up it was half a step back.

On and on, hour after hour, we continued to climb up the incredibly steep 45-degree slope of the ancient volcano. It became a matter of simply putting one foot in front of the other, while the bitter wind chilled us to the bone. The higher we climbed, the thinner the air became—so thin that all of us were breathing heavily just to move one foot at a time. It was a slow, monotonous rhythm—step up one foot, breathe deeply, step up another foot, breathe deeply. On and on we climbed in the darkness. At one point, as we neared the summit, two of our group felt totally exhausted and couldn't get their breath. But after a short stop, the rest of us encouraged them to persevere. Just as we approached the rim of the giant volcanic crater atop Kilimanjaro, the early morning sunrise began as a soft warm glow across the entire eastern horizon of the earth—what looked like half of the world! At last we stepped on to the edge of the crater rim, a place known as "Gilman's Point" at 18,500 feet elevation. From there, as we looked east toward the sunrise, we knew we were the special guests of GOD, and with the best seats in the house! As we watched from the top of Kilimanjaro, the soft orange glow on the horizon became brighter and the clouds below us reflected the sun's early rays.

Sunrise from summit of Mt Kilimanjaro

Then, the climactic moment arrived as a massive ball of fire slowly rose over Mawenzi Peak below. The jagged rocky spires appeared to be on fire, as if they were giant burning candles, sending the brilliant sunlight skyward and into the heavens! The entire peak was glowing with fire—a spectacular and awesome natural phenomenon as anything I had ever witnessed before in my life! As the sun began its daily journey westward, I knew I had been most fortunate to have shared the experience. Having reached Gilman's Point, the official summit of the climb, we turned to face the west and looked down into the massive volcanic crater at the heart of Mt Kilimanjaro. As an ancient volcano, it had been dormant for tens of thousands of years. Snow and ice covered the floor of the crater and remnants of massive glaciers surrounded the rim. Our guide invited three of us to hike up a mile or so around the rim to "Uhuru Point", the highest point on Mt Kilimanjaro at 19,380 feet.

Me on the summit of Mt Kilimanjaro

Slowly we hiked along the southern edge of the crater, past ancient glaciers and spectacular ice formations, which Earnest Hemingway referred to as the "snows of Kilimanjaro", seen from the plains far below. But what most people thought of as a "snow covered" summit, was in fact the remains of ancient glaciers formed tens of thousands of years ago when the earth was in the middle of an "ice age".

As we approached Uhuru Point, we passed close to one of the ancient glaciers, and I was able to see the beautiful, deep blue color in the massive ice, in hundreds of layers formed thousands of years ago. The solid wall of ice towered over 100 feet above us as we gradually made our way to its base. When we stood at the foot of the massive glacier, its face was virtually vertical—a result of "sublimation". At such an extreme altitude, the ice did not "melt", rather it transformed directly from a solid form to water vapor! Such a unique natural phenomenon, and only on the top of Kilimanjaro. When we neared Uhuru Point, the bitterly cold wind became so strong it was difficult to remain standing upright. But we pressed on, one step at a time, until we reached the highest place in all of Africa—19,380 feet above sea level. We hugged each other, much in the same way as I suspected climbers on Mt Everest had done upon their conquest. From Uhuru Point we had the most awesome view of Tanzania, Kenya, and the plains of East Africa! There was no doubt at that moment—"everything" was below us! There was no higher point on the African continent, and it was a once in a lifetime feeling of literally being "on top of the world". (one would have to travel over 3800 miles to the Hindu-Kush region in Pakistan to find a higher place on earth! We marveled at the view of the world from almost 20,000 feet above sea level, at least for as long as we could bear the brutal cold wind.

Then we began our descent past the ancient glaciers that glistened as they reflected the brilliant mid-day sun. At one point, I took a photo of Tim standing at the base of a glacier that towered over 100 feet above him.

Tim standing next to Kilimanjaro glacier

At last we met up with the rest of our group at Gilman's Point and began our descent down the steep slope we had labored so hard to climb in the middle of the night. Whereas we had struggled to put one foot in front of the other on the climb up to the summit, we literally "plowed" our way down through the soft volcanic "scree", as if we were in deep snow. As we almost "flew" down the mountain, I couldn't help wondering how on earth we had been able to climb the incredibly steep slope in the middle of the night? As I looked back on the climb, I was sure that one of the main reasons for climbing the steep ascent during darkness was psychological, so that what might otherwise look "impossible" would not stare us in the face for the five long hours required to reach the summit. And, of course, there was another important reason for the night climb—to arrive on the summit at the precise moment of sunrise over Mawenzi Peak! It was truly a joy to witness the spectacle of sunrise from atop Mt Kilimanjaro, knowing we were the first people to see it in all of Africa that morning! Within a couple of hours, we arrived back at Kibo hut, where our porters had prepared hot soup to welcome us and celebrate our successful climb.

A short time later, we began the long 10-mile hike down to Horumbo hut. Somehow, the cold wind that swept the broad barren ridge between Kilimanjaro and Mawenzi didn't seem as bitter or uncomfortable as it had felt before. Perhaps we were becoming accustomed to the altitude and mountain climate. We arrived at Horumbo hut in the late afternoon and the air quickly became very chilly as clouds began to fill the sky. As we settled down in the hut, I met a girl from Finland who would be going up to the summit the next morning. I asked her about her hometown and when she said she was from Helsinki, I mentioned I had gone to graduate school with a guy from Helsinki named Rikko Haarla. Immediately she gasped and said he was her friend! Then she told me he was working in the southern part of Tanzania—it was a very strange coincidence and really amazing. I ended up lending her a few of my clothes for the climb.

Then I walked down to a small mountain stream for a quick washup before dinner. It turned my whole body into a giant goose bump, but it was also very refreshing and invigorating! I joined everyone for a wonderful dinner of roasted beef, potatoes, carrots, and hearty vegetable soup—it was clear that my appetite had returned in earnest. As the evening fell upon the mountain, we sat around the table in the hut playing cards, reading, and swapping stories with those who had been to the summit (aka "veterans"), as well as those awaiting their chance (aka "neophytes"). Later that evening, as the oil lamps were turned out, I fell into a deep sleep, anticipating the return to base camp the next day. My last thoughts were of my love for Marion and the prospect of her letters waiting for me in Mombasa!

[**Day 5**] We were awakened early, once again by our ever-faithful guide named John, who always brought us hot tea to give us the energy and motivation to climb out of our warm sleeping bags. Following another hearty breakfast, and a bit of first aid on my heel blisters, we set off down the trail. Tim set a quick pace as both of us "scrambled" down the path, but we were certainly no match for our porters who seemed to "zoom" past us in their eagerness to return home and be with their families. About a mile down the trail from Horumbo hut, we encountered smoldering ashes and a landscape scarred by the huge brush fire we had seen several days before. The blackened earth seemed to stretch for miles in front of us, almost all the way to the rocky base of Mawenzi Peak. We scurried through the charred land, and surprisingly, amid the devastation were several small pools of standing water from a storm the night before. So, I figured it must have been the rain that doused the flames and saved part of the mountain from a worse fate. I recalled having seen storm clouds boiling over Mawenzi Peak when I had sat on the rocky point near Horumbo hut on our ascent up the mountain. It seemed that nature had prevailed in the end, as it always must.

Further down the trail, we came upon a couple of hamster-like animals that appeared to have been "stunned" by the fire—they just sat in front of us with blank eyes! They were the unfortunate innocent victims of human carelessness. Beyond the fire zone, we reached the thick forest, which had been too moist to burn and most likely acted as a natural "fire break". And just as soon as we entered the forest of lush vegetation and moss hanging from the trees, the soft light of the sun filtered through the dense canopy of thousands of leaves. A couple of miles further, we arrived at Mandara hut in time for lunch, which had been prepared by our porters well before our arrival. As we sat on the porch of the hut, enjoying our boiled eggs, biscuits, and crisp fresh carrots, I began to compose stories in my head of our ascent to the summit of Mt Kilimanjaro. Although I was certainly not the first person to reach the summit, it was still an astounding personal achievement none the less. And at that moment, now on the descent, I felt incredibly proud of having achieved my goal! But even more importantly, the experience of reaching the summit was one of a lifetime that would stay with me forever! It was a short lunch stop, after which Tim and I hurried down the trail for the final 12 miles to the national park entrance gate, the place where we had started our trek to the summit of Mt Kilimanjaro five days earlier.

Upon reaching the gate, we each wrote a few comments in the visitor's book about our experience. But quite frankly, even though I tried hard, I found it difficult to put my amazing experience and deep emotions into words on paper. As I attempted to compose a few sentences for the record, they seemed hardly adequate to express my deepest feelings and emotions—but how could one expect to do so with only a few lines on paper? However, I did chide the National Park Service for their proposed road construction all the way to Mandara hut. I was just glad I had been able to hike to the hut without the ugly sight of a road. As we prepared to leave the national park, we had our guide take a photo of us as we all stood beside the entrance sign.

Mt Kilimanjaro climbing party - Tanzania

(the equivalent of a modern day "selfie") We were clearly back to civilization again as we trudged down the road for the final 3 miles, past many people, houses, cars, etc. until we reached the hotel. While we sat in the lounge with cold beers in hand, we all shared the same good feeling of having reached the summit— but it also felt good to be back down. Sharing the experience around the roaring fireplace with friends, I felt a strong inner emotion of satisfaction and peace with myself.

As other climbers arrived, we celebrated our "comradery", now being mountain climbing "veterans", with another round of cold "White Cap" beers. But it was short-lived when the "little Hitler" from the Kibo Hotel suddenly showed up to demand extra money from Bill and Petra, in the name of the National Park Service, for having overstayed their permits. (they had paid only for permits as far as Kibo hut, not to the summit)

They were required to pay a fine of 55 schillings each. Despite the clear evidence from the guide, both of them became very defensive and rather nasty about it, refusing to pay the fine, even though they were well aware of being in the wrong.

At that point, each side became unreasonable, and it resulted in a lot of shouting—the whole scene was very embarrassing for the rest of us. In my opinion it was totally uncalled for on the part of Bill and Petra. Finally, as the local police arrived and threatened to haul them off to jail, they paid the fine! It was a most regrettable ending to an otherwise very beautiful and incredible journey to the summit of Mt Kilimanjaro. So, we quickly split from the ugly scene and headed for Twiga Beach. Along the way we dropped off Bill in the small town of Voi where he could hitch a ride to Nairobi. Then we drove on into the late afternoon toward Mombasa and the south coast of Kenya. That evening, we shared dinner at the "Curry Bowl" and talked about some of our most memorable moments on the climb to the summit. After dinner, we checked into the "Savoy Hotel" for the night in downtown Mombasa. Unfortunately, the water had been turned off earlier in the evening, so there was no shower that night. But I did manage to scrounge up a wash from a bucket of water in the toilet. Needless to say, it was rather inconvenient, but what could one expect for 7 schillings a night? (about $1.25) We had gone from the snows of Kilimanjaro to the oppressive heat of a Mombasa night, all in the same day! Such was the incredible diversity of Africa!

February 20, 1975
Mombasa, Kenya - Twiga Beach

"*Between Hello and Goodbye*" At 5:00am I was rudely awakened by chants from the Holy Koran over a loud-speaker directly above my window. So, I decided it must be time to take a shower and clean-up after 5 days on the trail. When I returned to my room, Tim told me my friend had been there earlier, looking for me. As I started to go downstairs to ask the hotel manager where my friend had gone, I spotted someone sprawled on the bed in the next room. Sure enough, it was John! I immediately awakened him with a loud "Good Morning" and a hearty handshake. Then we headed to a small café around the corner to have breakfast and a long conversation about our exploits over the past 10 days. It seemed that John's trip to Dares-Salam and the island of Zanzibar had been a real disappointment. He found very few things of interest, and travel around Zanzibar was very restricted, so much so that he felt like a captive. So, he ended up flying back to Nairobi after only three days. His disappointment was made even worse when I described my fantastic trip to Mt Kilimanjaro. I could tell he was filled with envy. Later, he told me he had put down a deposit of 400 schillings on a ticket for the boat to Bombay leaving that afternoon! So, it was now certain he would be leaving Africa and going to India, in a matter of a few hours.

Once again, he asked if I would join him, and once again, I had to refuse. I knew he desperately wanted me to travel with him, just as much I wanted him to stay—but neither of us forced the issue any further. After a final cup of coffee, we went about the business of picking up his ticket and making final arrangements for the long 11-day voyage. When we arrived at the travel agency, they refused to give him the ticket at first, claiming he hadn't paid the balance due on time. But after considerable "pleading", they assigned him a berth (bunk on the ship. Then he went down to the shipping company to get his ticket stamped, while I stopped by the bank to exchange some traveler checks, before returning to the hotel to wait for him. Thankfully, John had picked up my mail the day before, and I immediately set about reading it. I sat on the front steps of the hotel, and as I opened my first letter from Marion, my hands trembled, and my heart pounded—I was unaware of everything else around me. Her letter was so warm and touching—my eyes scanned each and every one of her handwritten words. And at that moment, I felt all my emotions well up inside me—it was as if I could almost hear her talking to me! Her letter reassured me of her love, and I felt thoroughly at peace! Then I read letters from family and friends back home. It was especially nice to receive a letter from Joan and my housemates in Seattle, along with a photo of them seated around the fireplace. I had missed them many times during the trip.

After quite some time, John came rushing into the room, grabbed a quick shower, picked up all his worldly possessions, and we headed for the dock. Along the way, we stopped at the Curry Bowl for a quick bite of lunch, and a final conversation about our plans, our friends, and the best moments we had shared in Africa. There was a definite touch of sadness in the air as we talked about going our separate ways. Neither of us had any feelings of regret about our decisions, and I wished my dear friend all the best, wherever his travels might take him—he wished me the same. Then we caught a taxi that took us to the port and arrived just in the nick of time for John to clear customs before the final boarding call. The entire dock was packed with people seeing their friends and relatives off on the voyage. At that point, John and I were sort of lost among the masses. I had been hoping to visit the ship and see John's home for the next 11 days, but by that time, there was no way to do so. In a last minute rush, reminiscent of my time at Nairobi airport to see Marion off to London, I bid a fond farewell to my best friend, with a warm embrace and a hearty handshake—I let go of his hand at the last possible moment as he climbed aboard the gang plank with his bright yellow backpack, bumping into masses of people. I stood on the dock, along with a thousand other people, and chatted with John aboard the ship as best as I could in the last few minutes before the ship's horn sounded and the gang plank was hauled up. Slowly the ship was moved out of its berth and into the main channel. It was my first sight of a large ocean-going passenger liner leaving port, and it seemed to be in slow motion compared to any other form of transportation—fascinating!

Ever so slowly the huge ship steamed out of the harbor, and I waved a final goodbye to my best friend. (I knew not where or when we would meet again, but as fate would have it, we would meet again on a very auspicious date that neither of us knew about at that moment!) As the ship sailed out of sight, I left the dock and joined my Kilimanjaro mates for the return to Twiga Beach Lodge, our original meeting place 10 days earlier. I looked forward to a period of rest and recuperation, as we were all suffering from blisters and aching muscles. We pulled into Twiga Beach campground late in the afternoon and found all our gear still in place and accounted for, exactly as we had left it 10 days ago! It was an amazing testimony to the honesty and integrity of the campground residents. I pitched a small shelter next to some rocks on the beach, just in case there might be a morning rain shower. Later that evening, as the sun was setting, I walked along the beach and found a straw mat that had washed up on the sand. It became the floor for my shelter at night and my sunbathing mat during the day. That night I was lulled to sleep by the soft, soothing sound of the waves caressing the sand on the incoming tide.

February 21- 26, 1975
Twiga Beach Lodge, Kenya

"Time to Myself at Twiga" The following morning, I awoke early with the sunrise, as would be the case each morning during my time at Twiga Beach. I began the day with a walk along the beach, inspecting the debris left overnight by the outgoing tide. The day was pleasantly warm, with a constant, refreshing breeze from the sea. Soon, I discovered the "intertidal zone" and some fascinating tide pools, of which I had read about in Rachel Carson's book. As I slowly waded through the shallow water and among the seaweed, I saw countless numbers of minute sea creatures living their busy lives in a world so alien to mine. There were starfish, mussels, crabs, snails, sea worms, small tropical fish of all colors, and thousands of other animals and plants too small to see. That day, Rachel Carson's book came to life as I stood hovering over the tidal pools. At times, I could recognize some of the tropical fish I had only seen in fish tanks before. I must have spent several hours roaming the turbulent, dynamic tidal world, silently watching the wonder of sea life at my feet, squirming between my toes at times, going about their daily life. I was like a giant in a miniature underwater world! Back on the beach, little sand crabs scurried out of their burrows in the sand and ran down to the water's edge in search of food, playing a game of tag with the surf. As the tide rose higher, their burrows were quickly submerged, and they immediately began to dig new ones. It was a constant task they performed day after day, year after year!

Returning to the open-air café at the lodge, I settled in for a coffee and some writing in my journal, as well as letters to friends and family. I would often sit there for hours at a time, engaged in my literary pursuits, as the warm ocean breeze gently ruffled my hair. Time passed by silently, without my notice, until evening drew near and my thoughts turned to dinner. It was always a very pleasant evening as people gathered amid the rustic surroundings of the lodge under a beautiful full moon. A gentle ocean breeze weaved its way through the lodge as the surf quietly swept the beach.

Twiga beach lodge - Kenya

The residents of Twiga Beach included a large group of overland travelers who had been camped on the beach for several months, and some had even built makeshift structures among the palm trees, resembling "beach houses". They were obviously there for an indefinite period of time, and I found many of them to be rather insensitive to the world of the sea around them. For these people, Twiga Beach was just a place to lie around all day and get stoned. They also liked dressing up like natives and were primarily interested in "passing time" with a minimum of physical effort or mental strain. They were nice people, but so mellow and laid back, to the point where they let days pass without concern for anything outside of their little world they had created on the beach.

After a while, I came to believe that reality, rather than time, was passing them by! As for my time, it was filled with hours of quiet, relaxed reading, writing, and study of the sea around me. There was also time to contemplate my future, as I lay under the warm sun and blue sky. However, a couple of days after arriving at Twiga Beach, I developed a badly chapped and slightly frost-bitten lower lip, as a result of the climb to the summit of Kilimanjaro. My lip became worse as the days rolled by, to the point where the skin broke apart in several places and developed a serious bacterial infection. Quickly, my lower lip swelled to three times its normal size, and for the next few days, all I could feel was its huge size and constant pain. It was extremely sore and very painful whenever I moved my mouth, even slightly. For two days I couldn't eat anything solid, as it would rupture the sores, further complicating and delaying the healing process. Unfortunately, and most frustrating, was the fact that speaking was made difficult and very painful.

And on the occasion when I had to say something, it felt as if a sharp knife was poking through my lip. Sometimes, I was certain it must have also looked painful to the people around me. I felt awkward as I walked around the lodge, knowing everyone must have been staring at me with eyes of amazement and pity for my swollen and frost-bitten lip. But there were also times when I almost forgot about the lip, until by accident, I touched it with the edge of a glass of juice or beer. Instantly, I was made aware of its presence! Liam was kind enough to lend me some antibiotic paste to put on my lip, and it began to heal quickly. But I was left with a "reminder" of it for the next couple of weeks. In retrospect, the beautiful, quiet, reflective moments at Twiga Beach were "balanced" by times of pain and anguish from the "lip"!

February 26, 1975
Twiga Lodge to Nairobi, Kenya

"A Time to Move On" After spending several days on the beach, I was anxious to return to Nairobi and check the Post Office for letters from home, and especially letters from Marion. Before leaving Twiga Beach, Liam had asked me to meet one of his friends in Nairobi visiting from Washington, DC. She wanted to go to some game parks around Nairobi. I agreed to meet with her and help her to make arrangements. That morning I was lucky enough to find a couple of Dutch guys who were going to drive to Nairobi, so I invited myself along. We spent the morning in Mombasa running errands and then headed northwest on the main highway to Nairobi. The route took us through Tsavo National Park, where we spotted several large herds of elephants, for which Tsavo is most famous. Upon arriving in Nairobi, I checked into the Hill Station Lodge, cleaned up, and walked uptown for dinner at my favorite place, the Bamboo Shoot. It was filled with so many wonderful memories, as well as being a fantastic dinner experience.

After dinner, I checked out the cinema, but found the offerings to be uninteresting and rather disappointing. So, I headed for the Thorn Tree Café to have a cold Tusker beer. As I was enjoying the beer, I spotted Joe and some of his overland passengers from the ill-fated SIAFU trip that was supposed to have left Nairobi two weeks earlier. It was their last night in town before heading to the Sudan, in hopes of traveling through the country to Egypt. But Joe still had not been able to secure the necessary road permits. However, he said he would be taking several cases of beer in the hope of bribing the Sudanese border officials. As I listened, I had serious doubts about the wisdom of his strategy, but as we parted, I wished him success and a safe journey. His group had already experienced more than their fair share of adversity, and now faced more potential problems ahead. But such were the hazards and challenges of overland travel in Africa. (I never did hear if they made it to Egypt or not)

CHAPTER NINE

February 27–March 1
Nairobi

"*Once again in Nairobi*" or "*Where to go From Here*" I awoke to the familiar sounds of a dog barking, baby crying, trucks loading, sewing machines sewing, and the sound of a familiar voice asking for directions to the shower. As I listened more closely, I recognized the voice as that of a friend from Lamu days—it was Ray. I got up and went upstairs to the bathroom, where I found him shaving. We talked of things we had done and places we had been since leaving Lamu Island. Then he said he would be departing for London the next morning. Later, we met up at the New Stanley Hotel for coffee and lunch. Soon after, Bill from the old Kilimanjaro gang showed up and lamented his situation of being broke, not yet having received funds from his bank in New York. He was near the end of his rope, walking the streets of Nairobi during the day and sleeping in the Sikh Temple at night. Then I mentioned how reasonable was the cost of staying at the Hill Station Lodge. So, Bill decided to make the move and we ended up sharing a room. A bit later in the afternoon, Charles showed up and we shared news of what everyone from the days of Lamu Island were up to now.

Just as I was about to leave the café, Liam's friend Barbara came by and we began to discuss a plan to rent a car and visit some of the national parks west of Nairobi for a couple of days. Then she left to join a tour of nearby Nairobi National Park, and I spent the rest of the afternoon in the café writing letters and bringing my journal up to date. That evening, I met up with Bill and Ray for a few beers, before heading back to the Hill Station Lodge for a quiet evening of listening to music and reading letters from home again.

The next morning, Ray left for London, suffering from the effects of a serious hangover he acquired during his last night in town at the infamous "Starlight Club"! He must have boarded the plane still feeling sick and unable to keep anything down for very long. It would likely be very frustrating for him when the stewardesses served food and drink throughout the flight. I spent much of the afternoon in quiet contemplation as I read the letters from Marion again. I sensed her feeling of loneliness and dissatisfaction with being back in England. I also had the same feeling of loneliness, even though I was among a group of friends with whom I had travelled in Africa. During the past four weeks we had been apart, I had constantly thought of her, and the realization of my deep affection and love for her was suddenly staring me in the face! As I sat in the Thorn Tree Café, with her letters in my hand, I reflected back on the beautiful times we had shared on the journey across Africa and especially the month living together on Lamu Island.

At that moment, the longing to be with her again became like a pain in my heart. With my dearest friend John off to India for several months, and the conditions of travelling north through the Sudan and Ethiopia to Egypt being bad, I suddenly asked myself, "why should I stay in Africa any longer if where I really wanted to be was in London with Marion"? Sitting in the café, as I had done countless times before, I quickly made the decision. I leapt up from the table and literally ran to the travel agency where Marion and Ginny had booked their return flight to London a few weeks before. As I stepped into the office to enquire about charter flights to London, I was told it wouldn't be possible to book a flight earlier than the end of April, almost two months away. The news sent my hopes straight downhill! Then the agent said, "come back in a few days and check for a cancellation". As I walked out of the office, I wondered if there might be other charter flights available, so I began checking around downtown and ended up at the Simba Airlines office. They directed me to one of their agents, and to my great joy, I was able to book a flight to London, departing Nairobi on March 12th, for only 1800 schillings ($275.00)!

With confirmed ticket in hand, I walked back to the New Stanley Hotel to celebrate the impending return to my love in London. My spirits soared as I imagined how our reunion might be, and I couldn't wait to write a letter to her about the news! That day in Nairobi was a beautiful day and I was so happy about my decision. Later in the day, Barbara came by and we discussed the plan to leave the next morning for a trip to the region around Mt Kenya. We had dinner in the café, and that evening she insisted upon going to the cinema. The movie was "Airport 75", a spoof about an airliner collision where the hero (Charleton Heston) accomplishes an incredible and truly bizarre stunt of being lowered from a helicopter into the empty pilot's seat of a 747 travelling at 180 mph! If the acting was lousy, which it definitely was, the stunt work was outstanding!

The next morning, after another night of noise from dogs barking, trucks loading, and sewing machines sewing, all at the same time, I woke up. Following breakfast, I hurried to the Post Office to see if there was another letter from Marion, and there I ran into Liam who had just come back from Mombasa. When I told him of my travel plans with Barbara, he said he had been thinking of travelling to some of the national parks in the north of Kenya—and maybe we should work out something when Barbara and I returned to Nairobi. In the meantime, I received a message from Krem that he was back in town after having finished his mining job in southern Kenya. I knew he would check the Thorn Tree Café to see if I was there, and sure enough, we met up. Over a cup of coffee, he told me about his experience of working in the mine and the appreciation he gained for the local miners who toiled six days a week for little more than subsistence pay. But unfortunately, there was nothing he could have done to change the situation.

Then Barbara showed up to talk about our travel plans for the next couple of days. After some discussion, all three of us decided to rent a car for three days and visit the region around Mt Kenya, before joining Liam for a trip to the national parks of northern Kenya. So, Barbara rented a VW beetle that afternoon and we headed out of town toward Mt Kenya. Barbara insisted upon driving, which became a source of frustration for Krem and me, as she refused to change to lower gears going up hills. Not wishing to be a "back seat driver" and make her nervous, I restrained myself from screaming at times. But after a while, I had to "offer" a few "suggestions" about shifting gears when she asked why the car was so slow going uphill (duh!). She was one of those people with no mechanical aptitude. That evening, we drove into the small town of Embu, looking for a place to have dinner. Our first stop was the famous "Issac Walton Inn". While it was stunningly beautiful, it was also much too expensive for our budget. The inn was world renowned for fantastic trout fishing in the streams of the foothills surrounding Mt Kenya. We drove through the entire downtown Embu, which wasn't saying much, to check out the local eateries.

Finally, among the grungy places was a boarding house that had a halfway decent patio, where we ordered some food and beer. When the food arrived, we were flabbergasted at the sight of a large mountain of chips covering almost the entire plate. (it seemed wherever we went in Kenya, everything came with chips!) As we stuffed ourselves with potatoes, we began thinking of finding a place to sleep. Krem and I checked on various options for lodging in town, but found all of them fully booked, due to a big dance and festival in town. We walked up and down the dusty, dim lit main street, but with no luck. So, we headed out of town to find a field alongside the road in which to roll out our sleeping bags. About three miles north of town, we spotted a little dirt road off to the left and we turned in. We found ourselves in the middle of a coffee and tea plantation. We pulled up in a steep lane and parked on the edge of the dirt road. Barbara quickly claimed the privilege of sleeping in the car, since it was pretty obvious that she had little experience sleeping out under the stars. Krem and I rolled out our sleeping bags under the coffee trees, with a billion stars shining above us. It seemed as if I had just fallen asleep when I was suddenly awakened by the sound of voices.

As I came to a conscious state of mind, I heard someone ask, "but why do you sleep in the bush?" Then came Krem's response, "because we like it here". Again, the voice asked. "but why do you sleep in the bush? If you need a place to stay, I can take you to the Police Station, they let you sleep there". It was obvious that the man was drunk and quite incapable of understanding the concept of "camping". It must have been completely incomprehensible to him, that we of all people would want to "sleep in the bush". Finally, the drunken man tired of his efforts to persuade us to go with him to the Police Station and moved on into the night—much to our joy! We settled back into a deep sleep among the coffee trees, under the stars, and caressed by the gentle night air.

March 2-3, 1975
Embu – Meru – Nanyuki - Aberdare National Park

"Into a Land of Spectacular Waterfalls" We awoke with the rising sun to find ourselves in the middle of a region covered with coffee, tea, and banana farms. We packed up our gear and drove back into the small town in search of breakfast. Krem suggested the Issac Walton Inn and we savored a delicious buffet on the outdoor deck that would last us all day. Following the very relaxed and enjoyable breakfast, we drove some very scenic roads around the base of Mt Kenya, through beautiful steep valleys to the town of Meru. There we stopped for petrol and a coke at the "New York Bar", before continuing our journey around the north slope of the mountain, whose 16,350-foot summit was cloaked in a veil of thick clouds. As we continued around the base of the mountain, the landscape slowly changed from open forest and meadow to vast expanses of grassland, turned a golden brown by the dry season. The grasslands seemed to stretch over rolling hills all the way to the horizon, much like one would see on the Great Plains of North America. Scattered among the hills were small wheat farms and cattle ranches, a scene I wasn't expecting to see in Kenya. But the northeast facing slopes of Mt Kenya were in the "rain shadow" of the mountain.

Mt Kenya

As we continued our journey among the foothills, we slowly returned to a much wetter environment of thick forest once again and drove into the town of Nanyuki. (little did I know at the time that I would later return to Nanyuki under very different circumstances) We encountered a brief, but intense thunderstorm as we left Nanyuki. It was the first significant rain since having been in Kenya for more than two months. Just beyond the small town of Nyeri, we turned off the highway on to a narrow dirt road that lead us uphill past a sign pointing to the "High Altitude Training Center for Olympic Games". We were on our way to Aberdare National Park, the site of the world famous "Tree Tops Hotel". However, that was not to be our destination for the night. Beyond the sign for the hotel, the road rapidly deteriorated into a rough track and became incredibly steep, such that the little VW bug just barely made it in first gear! As the road climbed higher, it twisted its way through an extensive forest plantation of Scotch Pine, mostly planted between 1958 and 1962. Above the plantation was a large expanse of bamboo forest that resembled a tall green fence on both sides of the road. Still higher, the road climbed into a scrub forest of small juniper brush and tall grasses.

Further on, we came to the crest of a long high ridge and the east gate to Aberdare National Park, at an elevation of just over 10,000 feet.

Entering Abedare National Park, Kenya

From that spot we had a spectacular view of the national park—a very high plateau of alpine moors and rolling hills covered with clumps of juniper brush. Looking to the west, we could see several rugged peaks of the Aberdare Mountain Range whose summits rose to more than 13,000 feet elevation. Upon entering the national park, the Ranger directed us to a campsite about six miles up the road, using a rough "hand-drawn" sketch of a map hanging on his office wall. After explaining the directions to us several times, unsuccessfully, he walked over to the wall, took down the map, and handed it to us! Leaving the park office, we followed a "squiggly" line on the map, up the road until we saw a tiny sign for "Quihara Campsite". As we pulled off the road, we found a small clearing among the juniper brush, where a couple of campfires had been established in the past.

After we unpacked our gear, I spent the last hour of daylight exploring the surrounding countryside of rolling hills and alpine moors. There were many small streams winding their way through the brush to places unknown. When I rounded a sharp corner on the trail, I saw another

210

small trail that lead to a stream below. As I made my way along the trail through the thick brush, I spotted a large antelope slowly moving up the trail toward me. So, I quickly stepped to the side and hid in the brush. The antelope disappeared below the slope, as I anxiously awaited its return to the trail. I sat quietly among the junipers for several minutes, and then suddenly, a large pair of antlers appeared in front of me—no more than six feet away! I sat motionless as he slowly walked toward me—I stared at him, almost in disbelief, not even blinking an eyelash for fear he would run away. Then, just as he was directly opposite from me, a distance no more than an arm's length, he abruptly stopped and looked me straight in the eye! And then, as if he had seen my frozen figure as somehow different from the juniper bush, he jumped back a couple of feet. Again, he stared at me, trying to determine if I presented a threat. Still wary of my presence, but certain he was in no immediate danger, he slowly walked on up the trail, occasionally looking back to check on me. It was one of the most incredible face to face encounters with wildlife and could only happen a few times in a lifetime! And where was my camera? Back in the car, of course! It was very disappointing, but I rationalized it by telling myself, if I had the camera with me, the antelope would never have been on the trail. But I would never really know for sure, though there might have been some truth to it.

Later that evening, the three of us huddled around a roaring campfire, thanks to Krem, and I shared my experience of the encounter with the antelope. The night was clear and very cold, as a billion stars showered us with a soft glow. The still of the crisp, quiet night was only occasionally broken by a soft rush of cold wind through the juniper bush above me. The next morning dawned clear and cold, with bright sunshine to greet us as we stumbled around, trying to start a fire and warm up. Slowly the rays of the sun began to penetrate our cold bodies and loosen our stiff muscles. For breakfast we cut up a fresh pineapple, and then moved out to visit the rest of the park. Our first stop, using the "homemade" map from the Park Ranger, was "Queen Cave Falls", a 45-foot-high waterfall hidden in a small canyon, surrounded by small palm-like plants—it was a lovely picnic spot. As we continued along the rough dirt road, I was pretty certain that it would become impassable during the rainy season.

We were in search of two massive waterfalls marked on the crude map and described in my Kenya guidebook. Eventually, after several false turns, we found the correct turnoff, but two miles further we were still unable to find the waterfalls. So, we doubled back and upon our return we spied the small directional sign at last. It pointed to a narrow footpath that led us down into a narrow canyon and across a small stream into some thick willow brush.

Then all of a sudden, we emerged from the brush into a small open meadow where there was a sign that read "Karura-Gura Waterfalls"! Just on the other side of the sign was the same small stream we had crossed over earlier, and a few yards further we came to the edge of a deep, narrow gorge. Suddenly, we found ourselves standing on the very edge of the "Karura Waterfall" as it plunged 1,000 feet straight down to the bottom of the gorge! As we looked across the enormous gorge, we saw the "Gura Waterfall" cascading 800 feet to the bottom. Further down the gorge the two streams joined forces to form a river that had cut a tortuous route between the sheer thousand-foot high cliffs on either side. It was a most impressive display of nature's power. Krem took a photo of me standing on the edge of the waterfall that plunged a thousand feet to the bottom of the gorge.

Standing at the top of Karura waterfall, Abedare NP

As I stood overlooking the deep chasm from atop the waterfall, it was a scary moment, but also a most inspiring sight. After witnessing the spectacle of the giant waterfalls, we drove up to the top of the ridge above the gorge and were rewarded with a fantastic panoramic vista of the snow-clad summit of Mt Kenya looming over the vast plains below. It was still early in the day, so there were very few clouds to obscure the view of its rugged spires rising over 16,000 feet above the plains. As we continued south through the park on the 10,000-foot-high plateau, we saw a small herd of antelope deftly dodging their way across the moors.

Eventually, we came to the west gate of the park, known as "Jerusalem Gate". There we stood at 11,000 feet elevation overlooking the "Great Rift Valley" 6,000 feet below us! We could see a hundred miles across the enormous trench to the "Mau Escarpment" on the other side, which was almost as high. The scene was one of the most impressive landscapes I had ever seen! Maps could never convey the enormous expanse of the Great Rift valley as accurately as the view we had that day. Slowly we weaved our way down the steep, twisting mountain road through thick bamboo forest and recently planted Scotch Pine plantations to the valley below. When we reached the valley floor, we looked up at the mountain from which we had just come, with a sense of having seen a part of Kenya that few people see.

Our route back to Nairobi took us through verdant fields of wheat and maize to the town of Naivasha, where we stopped at a small hotel for one of the typical Kenyan meals that always included a huge plate of chips. As we sat down to our lunch, Barbara decided to play a tune on the old "Rock-Ola" juke box sitting next to our table. No sooner had she sat back down than a tremendous blast of sound from the machine shattered our eardrums! The volume was so high, it was impossible to even yell across the table—what a big mistake! After finishing our meal, and being nearly deaf, we continued our return to Nairobi, pausing briefly at a lovely picnic spot on a rocky cliff overlooking the Great Rift Valley. Back in Nairobi, we turned in the rental car and headed to the Thorn Tree Café for a cold beer. As we sat down at a table, Bill happened to show up and lamented his sad story of still having received no money from home yet. We shared our adventures of the past two days with him before he scooted off to meet Charles for an evening at the infamous "Eckball Hotel". Meanwhile, Barbara kept hinting at the idea of seeing a movie that evening, so Krem and I gave in and said we would go with her. We ended up watching a tired film of Sam Peckinpah violence, after which we bid her goodnight. Then I walked back to the Hill Station Lodge for a quiet night of rest in a real bed.

March 4, 1975
Nairobi

"Back in Nairobi—Making Travel Plans" The next morning, I joined Barbara and Krem at the New Stanley Hotel. The plan was to meet up with Liam to discuss travelling north to Lake Rudolph (now Lake Turkana) and the national parks of northern Kenya. Liam was late, so I went to the Kenya Coffee House, where I thought he might be, and sure enough, there he was. After a short conversation about the trip with Barbara, we agreed to meet up with Barbara and Krem at the New Stanley Hotel to finalize the travel arrangements. Helga and Petra, the two German girls from the Kilimanjaro group, would also join us for the trip north. After a couple of hours, we finally managed to get everyone in the same place at the same time. Then we all agreed to leave for Lake Nakuru and Thompson's Falls the next morning. From there, Barbara would take a bus back to Nairobi to catch her return flight to DC. Once all the arrangements were made, we headed to the New Avenue Hotel for their famous all you could eat salad bar. On the way, I ran into Dominique of the old SIAFU trip. She was fresh from a Tsavo National Park safari, and we chatted for a few minutes, then wished each other well, as she would be flying back to London that night. We enjoyed an enormous lunch of delicious salads, and Krem returned to the buffet four times!

Following lunch, I spent the rest of the afternoon doing the coffee house circuit and quietly contemplating my future, thinking mostly of Marion, for she was to be my future. After writing many letters and updating my journal, I joined Liam and the girls for an enjoyable evening at the "Oasis Club" behind the Mayfair Hotel. We sat outside on the patio in the warm evening air with lots of other overland travelers.

As we downed several cold Tusker beers, we swapped stories of our adventures in Africa. Liam and I were able to persuade the chef to cook a couple of char-grilled hamburgers on his outdoor grill, and they were delicious! As I took my first bite, I realized what I had missed for the past seven months! At the end of the evening, I walked back to the Hill

Station Lodge and enjoyed a quiet night listening to my favorite music and reading letters from Marion again by candlelight. Eventually, I drifted into pleasant dreams, anticipating tomorrow's travel.

March 5, 1975
Nairobi - Lake Nakuru - Thompson's Falls

"Ten Thousand Flamingoes" It was an early morning wake-up call for a rendezvous with Liam and the gang at the New Stanley Hotel. After a last check for mail at the Post Office, we roared out of town, bound for Lake Nakuru. We bounced down the rough highway to the Great Rift Valley with the sounds of Santana reverberating throughout the old Land Rover. As we arrived at Lake Nakuru National Park, Liam boldly stepped up to the Park Ranger and declared we were all "residents" of Kenya, much to our disbelief! We were probably some of the most unlikely looking "residents" Kenya had ever seen, but we were "in like Flynn" at a much-reduced entrance fee. Our first stop around the edge of the huge lake was a spot known as "Observation Blind", where we watched several hundred white Pelicans from the hidden shelter as they bathed in a freshwater spring just a few feet away.

White Pelicans - Lake Nakuru National Park, Kenya

Then we drove up to the "Observation Tower", a sort of tree house on a high cliff overlooking a large bay where more than ten thousand pink flamingoes made the alkaline lake their ancestral home. The vast multitude of birds made the bay appear as if the water was a bright pink color. The scene was amazing and very unique—a natural phenomenon for which Lake Nakuru was world famous. From the observation post we had a spectacular view of the entire lake and surrounding landscape. Leaving the tower, we continued our journey around the southern shore and through a land of thorn trees and brush to a large expanse of grassland where Waterbuck and Bushbuck antelope grazed peacefully in the mid-day sun.

As we neared the edge of the lake again, we saw hundreds of Pelicans, Marabou storks, and Ebu, all of which took to flight at the same time as a large pink cloud of Flamingoes slowly passed over the lake. Then we were back in the bush again as we made the circuit around the lake, until we came to a sign pointing the way to "Baboon Cliffs Lookout". It looked intriguing, so we roared up the steep dirt road and came upon a small wooden shelter. From that point we had a spectacular panoramic view of the entire extent of the lake and the valley. The lake was dotted with large pink and white spots where tens of thousands of birds were gathered. As we gazed upon the scene, a small thunderstorm passed over the far shore of the lake, creating a grey curtain over the still water. As we made our way back down the road, we spotted a small Bushbuck antelope mother with three fawns beside her in a little clearing, just a few yards away. It almost seemed as if they were posing for a family portrait, as our cameras clicked away. The rare sighting of the antelope and the tens of thousands of birds made our visit to Lake Nakuru a very special and beautiful experience.

Leaving Lake Nakuru National Park, we drove north to Thompson's Falls, where we checked into a very nice campsite next to a rustic old lodge.

Lodge at Thompson's Falls, Kenya

The campsite had running water and plenty of firewood. The lodge was a beautiful old log structure from the early 20th century and built on the edge of the canyon overlooking the falls. It had massive ceiling beams and a couple of large stone fireplaces, each with a blazing fire. As we entered the main lounge, we saw several cages of colorful parrots, parakeets, and even a rare, exotic "Bird of Paradise". One entire wall of the lounge was glass, where we could sit with a cold beer and gaze upon a small collection of gazelle, antelope, gold-crowned Peacocks, and pink Flamingoes. It was like a private zoo right outside the window. Meanwhile, in the background, the soothing sound of classical music provided the perfect atmosphere for the 4 o'clock tea service as we sat beside one of the stone fireplaces. Quiet conversation over dinner in the rustic dining room took up most of our evening. Then we all headed to the campsite to find a comfortable spot to roll out our sleeping bags for the night.

March 6, 1975
Thompson's Falls - Maralal Lodge

"Up Close with Wildlife" Following a restful night sleeping under a small grove of pine trees, I went to the lodge for a shower, only to find the water lukewarm, at best. But it was still good to feel clean again, despite the abundance of goose bumps. As I sat in the dining room with my coffee and toast, reading the local newspaper, I noticed a large proportion of the news was devoted to sensational stories—everything from "Man kills baby while trying to beat wife" to "Man found stealing chicken heads"! For the most part, there was a lack of real news. But Kenya had two national newspapers, one of which devoted an entire "column" to international news. Not being interested in the latest murders or robberies, or the sports scores, I decided to visit the falls instead. I descended a steep, narrow stone staircase to the bottom of the small canyon - the base of Thompson's Falls. It was a very pleasant, relaxing place, but not a particularly spectacular sight when compared to the giant waterfalls in Aberdare National Park. I sat on a boulder and listened to the soothing sound of the water cascading down to the rocks below.

Later, back at the lodge, we gathered our gear and drove into town in search of a place to have lunch. As we looked around for a restaurant, we came upon the "Happy Bar and Restaurant". Inside we found the weirdest collection of "primitive" modern African art displayed on all the walls. There were scenes of daily life in Africa, all painted in bright, gaudy colors on a one-dimensional background, depicting events like riding a bus, a wedding, funeral, and so on. One scene was a strange piece of religious art showing GOD standing over a peasant farmer who had been turned into an ugly beast. Below the painting was the inscription, "Behold ye sinners, Repent your sins, Lest your punishment be like that of Nebuchadnezzar"! It was certainly enough to put the fear of GOD into most men! Having finished our lunch beneath the words of GOD looming above our heads, we piled into the Land Rover and headed north again. Soon we left the open woodland and entered the dry steppe landscape of northern Kenya, a sparsely populated region.

Late in the afternoon, we arrived at "Maralal Lodge" to deliver a cash receipt book from the manager of the Thompson's Falls Lodge. At Maralal Lodge we were treated to afternoon tea on the veranda. As we sat down, we had the good fortune of watching a herd of zebra, gazelle, and antelope grazing peacefully around a large waterhole in front of the lodge. They paid no attention to us and seemed quite at home— in fact, they acted as if they owned the place. It was an extraordinary experience to be sipping tea in the afternoon with 50 or 60 zebra just a few yards away! We sat on the veranda for several hours, watching as more animals came up to the waterhole in front of us. We also had a magnificent view of the vast African plains beyond as well. As dusk approached, we decided to spend the night at the lodge, and after asking the manager about camping, he offered us a tent with six cots for 7 schillings a piece. It was a great deal that we couldn't pass up. When we prepared dinner that evening, Petra discovered that of the 8 eggs we had bought in Nakuru, 6 were totally rotten, two of which were so bad they had turned a very sickly green color. The awful putrid odor from them was almost too much to bear before dinner! It was a major disappointment, but Petra managed to put together a tasty meal none the less.

Just as we finished dinner, a young Samburu boy came running to our tent, yelling that we must follow him. As we trailed after the young boy, who was clad in a wrap-around cloth and carrying a long spear, we all wondered what on earth he wanted to show us. All of a sudden, he stopped at the corner of the lodge and motioned us to be quiet. Then we all tiptoed around the corner and came face to face with a herd of Cape Buffalo gathered around the waterhole in front of the lodge. Quietly, we sat down on the veranda, along with the residents of the lodge, to watch the spectacle. It was an amazing sight under the light of the moon, almost as if we were watching a National Geographic documentary film. But it was real, and so was the sound of hooves stomping on the ground, the snorts from impatient bulls, and the pungent smell of buffalo dung in the air. The buffalo were still milling around the waterhole when we finally retired for the night.

March 7, 1975
Maralal - South Horr

"Off the Beaten Path" I awoke early in the hopes of seeing some new animals at the waterhole, but if they had been there earlier, they were now gone. However, the resident herd of zebra were back with their cousins, the gazelle and antelope. We enjoyed a leisurely breakfast on the veranda under the warming rays of the bright morning sun.

Breakfast at Maralal Lodge, Kenya

As we chomped away on our pancakes and eggs, the animals munched on the grass in front of us. As we marveled at the scene, we speculated about how much some people must have to pay to stay at Tree Tops Hotel to see the same thing we were seeing. The scene unfolding in front of us was truly authentic and simple—nothing staged for our benefit. It felt so natural, just another day in the life of Africa - we were privileged to be nature's guests that morning. Slowly the morning passed, and warthogs came to join the crowd at the waterhole. Finally, as the sun rose higher in the sky, we felt the urge to move on to the north. But before leaving, we drove into the small town of Maralal to buy petrol and stock up on some basic provisions. As we entered the town, we immediately became aware of the brightly colored dress worn by the people. Most of the women were bare breasted and wore large silver earrings and multicolored bead necklaces. The men also wore large silver ornaments, along with ostrich feathers in their hair. Some of them had small bells around their ankles and knees that gave music to their movement and created an exotic atmosphere as they went about their daily life. Looking down the dusty main street, with the sound of the bells and the colorful dress, I almost felt as if I was in the middle of a documentary film. But this was clearly everyday life in Maralal—the people weren't there to put on a performance for us. Having a full tank of petrol and some provisions, we drove north again on some pretty rough gravel roads that quickly became heavily corrugated, which made for a very hard, uncomfortable ride.

Time was moving on and our progress so slow, that by dusk we found ourselves in the midst of a thorn tree forest somewhere north of the small town of South Horr. So, we pitched camp among the trees and built a roaring fire. The evening was so still and peaceful, I was taken back to the beautiful nights in the Sahara Desert which I loved so much. I lay atop my sleeping bag beside the waning campfire, staring up at the infinite heavens and countless billions of glittering stars. The concept of time became almost meaningless at that moment. Sleep eventually overtook me as my last visions were of twinkling stars and the blackness of the night.

March 8, 1975
South Horr - Lake Rudolph

"The Biggest Fish I've Ever Seen" As had become my habit, I woke up with the rising sun and decided to spend some time exploring the surrounding country while everyone else slept. I walked up the dusty road to a dry riverbed—a "wadi", where I left the road to follow its course through

the trees. Soon, I was into a world of a thousand birds, all calling to the morning. Perched high in the uppermost branches of a large thorn tree were two huge vultures staring down at me. They were more curious than apprehensive, and they continued to trace my movement through the brush with their sharp, beady eyes. Further up the wadi, beneath the shadow of a high ridge, I flushed a whole quarry of birds that resembled partridge. There must have been 50 of them fluttering madly through the brush. All told, I must have seen at least a dozen different species of birds during the hour I tromped through the wadi. By the time I returned to camp, the rest of the group had begun to fix breakfast, and the wonderful smell of fresh toast and hot coffee was curiously mixed with the dry, dusty morning air. After a hearty breakfast, we continued our journey north toward Lake Rudolph. The road deteriorated rapidly into a single track and soon became little more than two thin parallel lines weaving their way among the boulders and lava rock strewn everywhere. It was a very rough ride, and Liam did an excellent job of navigating across the lava field.

As we neared the lake, we came to the top of a 1500-foot-high escarpment where we had a spectacular panoramic view of the enormous lake, which stretched north all the way beyond the border with Ethiopia, over 150 miles.

Overlooking Lake Rudolph - Kenya

As we gazed upon the lake below us, we were surrounded by lava rock and large boulders, with little, if any sign of vegetation. It was ironic that a huge freshwater lake could exist in such an isolated, barren landscape. Very slowly we wound our way down the narrow, twisting track, strewn with rocks, until at last we came to the shore of the lake. As we rumbled along the rocky road following the shoreline, we passed several flocks of pink Flamingoes and white pelicans, as well as several other kinds of birds that fished the lake. The lakeshore was as barren as the highlands above, and we slowly rumbled down the rough road for what seemed like hours, but in reality, probably no more than 30 minutes. Eventually we came to a small village and a large sign for the "Oasis Lodge". With our throats parched from the long, hot, dusty rough ride, we headed straight for the bar when we reached the lodge. The bartender served up ice-cold Tusker beers all around and we guzzled them down faster than he could make change. Then it was time for round two as we sank into the soft lounge chairs in the beautifully appointed lodge. The old lodge was surrounded by lovely palm trees, lush green grass, and had two swimming pools fed by a natural hot spring—a virtual Garden of Eden in the middle of barren sand and lava rock.

We spent most of the afternoon lounging by the pool, until a brief thunderstorm broke the calm as it passed quickly over the lake. That evening, a group of people who had flown in from Nairobi that morning, returned from a day of fishing on the lake. Their catch included some monstrous fish, one of which was a Nile Perch over 5 feet in length and weighed in at 128 pounds! It literally dwarfed the lady who had landed it, as she stood beside it for photos. On the wall above the bar was a board listing all the fish caught in the past year weighing over 100 pounds, and there must have been 25 or 30 on the list, the largest being 202 pounds! Had I not seen one with my own eyes, I would not have believed it. They more than matched that of many ocean game fishes. As an indication of their size, the "bait" were no small fish either, often being 5–10 pounds and 18–24 inches long. As I stood for a photo beside the 128-pound monster hanging next to the lodge, it was clearly "the biggest fish I had ever seen"!

Nile Perch from Lake Rudolph

We all stood around watching the cooks clean and cut up the fish. A single filet from one side alone took two people to carry it to the kitchen.

Finally, we could no longer resist the temptation to ask if we could buy some of the fish for dinner. After checking with the manager of the lodge, one of the cooks gave us five pounds for free, and even cut it into pan-size portions for us. Later that evening, Petra fried the fish in butter, garlic, and onion to make a dinner fit for a king! Of course, the dining room in the lodge featured Nile Perch on their menu as the specialty, but I was confident that our dinner rivaled theirs. Thoroughly "stuffed to the gills", so to speak, we went back up to the bar for a couple of cold beers before retiring for the night. As we drove out of the Oasis and past the sleepy village, we spotted a large open flat area with no rocks, only a mile or so from the lodge. So, we stopped and rolled out our sleeping bags next to the Land Rover and lay back to watch a fantastic display of brilliant stars above.

March 9, 1975
Lake Rudolph – Marsabit

"Night of the Scorpions" We awoke early in the morning to discover to our surprise, that we were perched on the end of the runway at the Oasis Lodge airstrip! No wonder it was so flat and free of rocks. Lucky for us, there were no early morning flights! As I got out of my sleeping bag, a strong gust of wind whistled past me, almost knocking me over. The wind was so strong, it was a hard task to get dressed. It was much too windy to even attempt cooking breakfast on the camp stove. So, we packed up our gear and moved on down the road. As we drove north, the condition of the track became a bit better, but that wasn't saying much. The day before, we had been told by some overland travelers at the lodge to be on the lookout for a shortcut that bypassed North Horr and saved many miles. It was said to be about half a mile beyond a "bad spot of sand". So, every time we spotted a bit of sand in the road, we looked for the "shortcut", anxious not to miss it. We passed through lots of sand on the road, but finally, as we rounded a sharp corner, there lay a long, curving pit of soft, deep sand, and we instantly knew this was it. Before anyone could shout "sand", the old red Land Rover was in the middle of a battle with the soft stuff, lurching, twisting, and flying through it! Sand and dust flew everywhere, up over the roof and in through the open windows, leaving us covered from head to toe!

226

Just as quickly as we had encountered it, we were back on solid ground, with only a thick layer of red sand to remind us of the "bad spot of sand". Then off to our right we saw the track we had been told about, as clear as day. On and on we roared across the sand and rock, until we came to an enormous dry salt lake bed that had the eerie appearance of being covered in fresh snow! For a brief moment, the optical illusion took hold of our minds, such that we felt a few degrees cooler. But the illusion was soon gone, and we were jolted back to reality by the rush of hot wind through the windows. As we continued across the barren land, there were a few times when we wondered if we had strayed from the main track, for it seemed a very long time to travel without seeing anyone or any sign of civilization.

Camel caravan crossing Chalbi Desert - Kenya

Then we passed a small oasis crowded with a herd of sheep and goats. Beyond the oasis was a mudflat so smooth it made us seem motionless as we drove across it. Once again, I harkened back to the days in the Sahara Desert when our vehicles would almost seem to fly across the sand, as if on ice skates. After a couple more hours, several metal and mud buildings appeared on the horizon, the first signs of a small village in the middle of nowhere.

As we drove into the tiny, dusty village, we became aware of all the people staring at us, as if we had come out of thin air. It was immediately apparent to us that tourists were a rare sight in this region. To our pleasant surprise, the village had a small bar and café, as well as a few shops along what appeared to be the main street. We parked the Land Rover in the middle of the village and headed straight for the bar. Warm beer was the only bill of fare, so that's what we drank. The little café next door served a limited menu, just tea and chapati, so that's what we ate. Soon, the whole village surrounded the Land Rover, trying to sell us whatever they had. At the same time, Helga and Petra danced the "bump" to the sounds of "Rock Your Baby" blaring at full volume from the stereo in the Land Rover. The local people got a real kick out of watching their performance, and some of them even joined the girls! It was a really happy time in Maikona that day. As we were leaving the village, I gave away all my writing pens, save for one, to the school kids who kept asking for them. It made me feel very happy that they were so overjoyed with such a small gift. The people of Maikona expressed a genuine interest in us as visitors in their village, not as tourists.

As we left the village, I couldn't help thinking about how fortunate I was to be able to travel and see the rest of the world, for these kids would never have that opportunity, nor would millions of others in the world. That day and our visit to the tiny village of Maikona would most likely be their only touch, however brief, with a world outside their own. For me it was an incredible eye-opening experience, seeing their excitement and joy, one that I would never forget! We drove on across the barren "Chalbi Desert", until at last, the volcanic hills of Marsabit loomed on the horizon. As we drove up to the foothills, life returned to the land in the form of grasses and brush. Then, as the road climbed into the hills, tall trees began to appear. When we reached the Marsabit National Park entrance, we entered a tropical forest at 5,000 feet elevation. The national park enclosed an ancient volcanic crater and was like an enormous oasis, surrounded by barren desert.

Landscape of northern Kenya

After entering the park, we stopped briefly at the old lodge for a cold Tusker beer. On one wall of the bar was a photo of the elephant with the world's largest tusks. Afterwards, we proceeded through the dense forest on a narrow, winding road, we passed a group of monkeys in the trees, as well as a troop of baboons and a small herd of gazelle. Eventually, we came to an overlook above Lake Paradise, where a herd of large bull elephants were bathing. The lake had been formed in the bottom of the crater thousands of years ago. As we neared the lake, we spotted another Land Rover that beckoned us to pull up alongside. They told us the herd would soon pass very close to us as it left the lake. We waited quietly, watching the huge beasts splash water and mud everywhere. Then one by one, they moved toward us, grazing leisurely on the shrubs as they went, until they were only 50 feet from us, to scratch themselves on a giant boulder.

Elephants in Marsabit National Park, Kenya

We could clearly hear the grating sound of their rough hide against the abrasive rock. When they had all scratched themselves into oblivion, they slowly walked past us and into the dense forest. About the same time, another small herd appeared from the hill behind us, going at full speed for the lake. They were females with their young, some of whom could barely keep up the pace—one was so small it could have only been a few weeks old. We watched as the bathing routine was repeated, after which they lumbered off to the opposite side of the lake for a "dust bath".

It was getting dark by that time, so we bid farewell to the herd and drove up the road to the rim of the crater. Just as we were about to make a sharp turn, we saw a large herd of Cape Buffalo coming down the hill to the lake. They stopped dead in their tracks when they saw us, so we moved out of their way, and after a few minutes, they continued on their way. Just behind the buffalo were a couple of giraffes, apparently waiting their turn at the lake. We continued our drive, when all of a sudden, just around a bend in the road, a huge bull elephant was staring at us from the edge of the forest—a mere 3 or 4 yards away! As the herd began to move across the road, so did we—it would have been no place to challenge the elephants for the right-of-way. The experience was definitely my closest encounter with an elephant! Eventually, we made our way down the mountain and out of the national park, making sure we didn't get lost on the narrow dirt roads at night.

Once we reached the main road, we were back into a barren land of sand and scrub. A few miles later, we pulled off to the side of the road to set up camp and fix dinner, a delicious combination of tomato soup and the remainder of the fish from Lake Rudolph. As we sat around the campfire, Helga said she saw something dash across the sand in front of the Land Rover. When we searched the area with our flashlight, it was nowhere to be found. Moments later, Petra screamed that a scorpion was sitting beside Liam's bare foot. And sure enough, as we aimed the flashlight, there was a large scorpion over 3 inches long. My climbing boots did a job on the scorpion and we were in possession of a "trophy"! Instantly, we all looked at each other with the same question on our mind—how many of the ornery little 8-legged bastards were there around us?

Suddenly, it became very tense as each of us began thinking about how to get some sleep that night without becoming a victim of a scorpion's sting. Petra and Liam had dibs on the inside of the Land Rover, and Helga quickly claimed a spot on the top of the roof. That left Krem and me to find a place on the sand beside the road. I fashioned a makeshift hammock from my groundsheet and fastened it to the front bumper of the Land Rover. Krem was hoping his air mattress would keep the little devils away. Needless to say, it was rather an apprehensive night without much sleep for me and Krem. And to add to the excitement and fear, bats kept strafing us during the night! Either they were trying to get a closer look at us, or playing games with us—whichever, it was a bit unnerving, to say the least.

March 10, 1975
Marsabit - Nairobi

"The ISIOLO EXPRESS" Very early in the morning or was it very late at night - hard to tell since it was still dark. I woke up to the sound of bells clanging, the rumble of the earth beneath me, and a voice singing a strong rhythm. After a few moments, I realized it must be a herd of cattle being led by a herdsman whose singing was meant to reassure the cows in the darkness. Soon, the thunder of hooves rumbled toward me, and as they got within a few feet, I hoped they had seen me. Luckily they had, and as I raised my head, the herdsman shouted "Jambo" (hello in Swahili). Gradually the sound of bells, hooves, and the man's song faded back into the night. I dozed off once more before being awakened by the rising sun. I counted heads and found to my relief that no one had been carted off during the night by scorpions or bats. Following a quick breakfast on the side of the road, we headed south on the rough gravel road toward Samburu. Much of the route was through a vast expanse of lava fields and scattered brush, occasionally broken by an isolated range of hills that supported more abundant vegetation.

Near the village of Laikipia, we were fortunate to spot two relatively rare animals for the first time— the Reticulated Giraffe and Grevy's Zebra, both with distinctive markings that clearly set them apart from their "brothers" to the south. About an hour north of "Archer's Post", we passed the wreck of a yellow Romanian jeep that Liam recognized as belonging to a friend he had met at City Park in Nairobi.

On the road to Archer's Post, Kenya

We stopped to survey the scene, only to find the vehicle a total loss. (later we found out the driver and passengers had been hospitalized with serious injuries) An hour later we pulled into the small town of Archer's Post—merely one dusty street and a few shops. There, I was to part company with the group, since they were headed to Samburu National Park, while I had to be in Nairobi that evening to prepare for a flight to London in the next couple of days. As we all shared a beer at the one and only bar/café in town, I asked around the town about buses to Nairobi, but no one seemed to know when or if one would roll by. After having no success, I resigned myself to asking Liam if he would take me to Isiolo, the next town down the road, where I hoped to find some sort of transportation to Nairobi.

Meanwhile, Krem had flagged down a southbound Army Land Rover, to ask if they could give me a ride. They said they would like to offer me a lift but couldn't because they were transporting a dead body— that seemed reason enough for me. As we sat in the tiny bar finishing our warm beers, it was decided that Liam would take the rest of the group to Samburu Lodge and return to Archer's Post to take me to Isiolo, if I had not been able to land a ride in the meantime, which sounded great to me. So, I bid a fond farewell to my travelling companions of the past two months and gave Petra my one and only classical music tape to help her keep her sanity in between "Black Sabbath" and the "Rolling Stones". She had always enjoyed listening to my tape of the Brandenburg Concertos, most likely since Germany was her home.

My last glimpse of them in the dusty old Land Rover was from the front porch of the old ramshackle bar, where I remained with my warm bottle of Tusker beer. Except for a few old people and small children scurrying alongside the road, there was not a sign of life for miles around, as the hot wind played with the dust in the street. It was at that moment I began to feel a ping of pain deep down in my heart at the thought of leaving Africa behind in a couple of days. It was then that I knew for certain just how much I would miss Africa. But, the prospect of seeing Marion again soon occupied my thoughts. As I sat among the old wooden buildings and dusty streets of Archer's Post, my mind returned to reality as I began to wonder how I would get from Isiolo to Nairobi, and where would I stay the night if the old reliable Hill Station Lodge wasn't available? Nonsense—since when in all of my travels in Africa had I been stranded?

Liam's beckoning from the old red Land Rover brought me back to the present, and soon we were driving south toward Isiolo, roaring over the gravel, covering what I was sure must have been intended to be a road. Just south of Archer's Post, Liam stopped to pick up two young Samburu warriors who "talked" their way into our vehicle with their radiant smiles and long pointed spears. The Samburu closely resembled the Maasai people to the south in many respects to their physical features, as well as their culture. They were tall, slim people, very proud and friendly, yet with reserved expressions. I found them to be a constant source of wonder and speculation. After another hour or so, we dropped them off beside the road, in the middle of a vast expanse of scrubland that looked the same for a hundred miles in any direction—but for these guys, it was a very special place, their home! Finally, we saw the town of Isiolo on the horizon and soon found ourselves back into a sort of civilized place.

At the first petrol station where we stopped, amongst crowds of people milling around with mountains of cardboard boxes, and crates of chickens, there were some old wrecked trucks and buses. When I asked about buses to Nairobi, I was told the next scheduled bus going south to Nairobi would not leave until the next morning. At that moment, my hopes plummeted, but surely there must be other forms of transportation—perhaps taxis or private cars? "No, but you might be able to hitch a ride on a truck". Several trucks later, I was no closer to getting a ride to Nairobi. Meanwhile, I noticed many cars racing up and down the main street, honking their horns, stopping anywhere where people stood, including on the sidewalk, and then roaring off again. Small groups of people loaded down with all their worldly belongings tied up in flimsy cardboard boxes and covered in blankets, kept milling around in the shade of trees scattered along- side the main street.

At that point, it looked like my only option was to put my thumb to the wind. But, as Liam and I neared the other end of town, my eye caught sight of an old Peugeot station wagon sitting beneath a rusty old Texaco sign. Emblazoned on the side of the old car, in large, bright orange letters were the words "ISIOLO EXPRESS—Isiolo-Nanyuki-Nairobi". Could this be my next ride I wondered? Liam swung the Land Rover around 180 degrees and slid to a halt in front of a half dozen young black guys sitting on the porch of an old wooden shack, which appeared to be the Texaco service station. I asked one of the guys if the old station wagon went to Nairobi and got an affirmative nod from all of them. And would it leave soon? There was another nod from the group to say yes, and in fact, one guy went on to say it would leave right now! So off came my rucksack and I was invited to join them on the porch while they watched the owner work on the old car. After a hasty, but very sincere thank you and farewell to Liam, I took a seat on the creaky old boards of the porch to await the completion of repairs to the "taxi". I was assured several times that it would, of course, only be a matter of a few minutes before we would be ready to leave.

Meanwhile, the young men began to ask me questions, about my home, my travels, and my impressions of Kenya. Before long, a friendly conversation was born from their tremendous curiosity and lack of knowledge about the world outside Kenya. One time I was asked if I was a CIA agent, heaven forbid, and another time if I planned to travel to South Africa, to which I answered "No, because I disagree with the racial policies there". Then one young man said, "you are wise, because one day those people gonna die"! Several of them couldn't believe I had earned enough money to pay my own way to Africa. They were convinced the American government must have paid for my trip. It was a natural misconception, since they couldn't relate to such a thing being possible for an individual. After all, they didn't have the means to even travel to Nairobi, let alone America! An hour passed, and the old car still remained parked in front of us. "Are you a CIA agent?" asked another young man again. It seemed an unlikely question since these young guys knew very little about the USA and kept badgering me with questions. It just went to show how the CIA was known around the world. Finally, I asked them how much longer it was going to be before we could leave, and promptly got the reply "right now"! On African time, that could mean anywhere from 10 minutes to four hours.

But all of a sudden, a man covered in oil and grease popped up from underneath the rear of the car and shouted that he was ready to leave—and so was I! I threw my rucksack into the back of the station wagon and jumped into the seat behind the driver. Two of the young men who had "interrogated" me on the front porch of the old "Texaco shack", also climbed in and we roared off up the main street in a cloud of dust and blue smoke. Into the center of town we went, squealing tires around corners and playing tag with the pedestrians lining the street. Several times we came to an abrupt halt in front of a bar or store, while one of the young men in the car jumped out, ran in and shouted "Nanyuki, Nairobi". At other times, people would come "out of the woodwork" to hail our car to a grinding halt. Once in a while they would get in and ride around town for a few blocks before getting out again. Other times, they would just talk to the driver for a while. Three times, a young black woman got in next to the driver, rode around with us, and then got out again.

After half an hour of this "cruising the main street" routine, I demanded to know what was up and when we were going to leave for

Nairobi! I was told that we needed 10 more passengers who wanted to go to Nanyuki or Nairobi before we could leave town! At the rate of 2 or 3 people popping in and out of the car every five minutes, I figured it would be at least another 2 or 3 weeks! To add to the absurdity of my predicament, I became aware of several other cars "cruising" aimlessly around town, honking their horns, and shouting their destinations, which often included Nairobi. What a joke it all was I thought—would we ever get out of town? It seemed like four hours passed, but in reality, it was probably only one, as we continued to cruise around an endless circle of businesses and people standing on the street. Then, out of nowhere came 10 paying passengers, loaded down with all manner of "luggage". As the last man hopped in the side door, the old Peugeot station wagon shot out of town like a rocket, swaying to and fro with the weight of 14 passengers and countless bags and boxes tied to the roof. It was more than a bit cramped, as five of us in the middle row tried to "adjust" our positions to find a comfortable spot. Meanwhile, the "ISIOLO EXPRESS" bounced down the highway at 150 kph (90 mph), as the tires touched the pavement occasionally. Fortunately, I only felt the car's movement, without the anxiety of actually seeing the road. We were definitely leading the race, but I had no idea of what race it was. After posting what I was sure to be an incredible record for the fastest elapsed time for the first leg of the trip from Isiolo to Nanyuki (aka the race), we slid sideways into Nanyuki's main marketplace. Almost immediately, I was besieged by hawkers shouting "Nairobi".

Then, one guy grabbed my rucksack and hauled it over to his car. It looked like this was to be my next ride. I enquired about the time of departure, to which I received the inevitable reply, "right now". That meant I probably had time for a beer, lunch, and a bit of sightseeing! But, to be on the safe side, I stuck close to the driver. Finally, as other cars around the marketplace began to race their engines, we climbed into our car as well. This time two other guys joined the car, which meant we only needed four more passengers, or so I thought. Then, just as had happened in Isiolo, we began "cruising" up and down the main street in search of the elusive passengers. Once in a while we took a side street, just to vary the scenery. After a half hour of little or no luck, the driver dropped off his two "decoys". (people who make the car appear almost full, so as to attract passengers who believe it will depart sooner because it needs fewer additional people—a very tricky maneuver indeed!) Then we headed back to the main marketplace to begin the whole process again.

At that point, I expressed, in the strongest terms, my need to reach Nairobi by evening, fearing he was about to give up the journey. But, as luck would have it, he turned the car around and roared out of town towards Nairobi, with me as his only passenger. Naturally, one couldn't drive a "taxi" at less than the maximum speed of which it was capable, so we glided down the tarmac at 90 mph. No sooner had we left Nanyuki, than an overturned car appeared off the side of the highway around a sharp bend. It was an old Peugeot station wagon with its wheels still spinning in the air. As we flashed by, I got a glimpse of the name painted on its side, which spelled out "ISIOLO EXPRESS"! The driver slowed down to 70 mph to get a better look at the damage, and asked me if it was the same car I had arrived in? Sure enough, it was! I counted my blessings that it had dropped me off in Nanyuki. Back up to 90 mph, we continued our way south, with the tires touching the tarmac once in a while. I began to believe that all taxi drivers in Kenya thought the "East African Rally" lasted 12 months of the year and they were all in it to win—against whom I didn't know. Just outside the small town of Nyere, my driver flagged down an overloaded old Peugeot station wagon sitting alongside the road. With a shout in Swahili to the driver, he managed to keep it from roaring off. Astonishment and a bit of fear swept over me as I learned that the old wreck with 13 passengers and their massive load of baggage was about to take on a 14th passenger—namely "me"!

After lodging a feeble protest over the apparent lack of space, I was squeezed in between two huge black ladies in the row behind the driver, where I had no view of the road. All I could do was hope the trip would be a quick one, balancing the danger of a crash at 90 mph, against the more likely hazard of being squashed to death as the old car swayed from side to side! Luckily, it was a short 20 minutes to the first stop to dislodge some passengers. But, then to my amazement, they were replaced by more people. Once again, I found myself squeezed between the two heaviest people in the car, and unable to even see out the window. Although, judging from the erratic motions of the car, it was probably a blessing. As the light began to fade from the day, we continued to pick up more people and make more frequent stops. I began to wonder, if anyone was caught standing on the side of the road they would be immediately shoved into the car, regardless of how many had already been added? At one point, I attempted to do a head count and came up with 15, but they were only ones I could actually see—I wondered, how many others were in the car or hanging on the roof, I had no way of knowing. Long, stuffy hours passed as the game of "musical passengers" played on and on. The eternal question of how long it would last, and would we ever get to Nairobi, was always on my mind.

The slow, endless pace of travel became a stark contrast to what I had experienced earlier in the day at 90 mph. At times, I began to feel as if I had been nowhere else for the past several days other than in this confounded old wreck of a car! Then, lo and behold, a glow of city lights on the horizon gave me hope that we were finally approaching a place of sanity amidst the sea of frustration I had endured for so many hours. At that moment, I was certain we were near Nairobi, at last. We came into the city by way of a circuitous route through the northern suburbs, which I didn't recognize. Suddenly, I wondered if perhaps I wouldn't be able to direct the driver to my destination, the old reliable Hill Station Lodge. Or perhaps he had other plans for me? But I knew from my experience, the vast majority of Africans I had come in contact with were far above any questionable activities with overland travelers like myself. Finally, after having dropped off all the other passengers, the driver asked me where I wanted to be dropped off. By some stroke of luck, he knew the Hill Station Lodge very well, and even commented on my good choice of reasonable accommodations—not like the "tourists" at the Hilton.

With a grateful thank you, I bade him farewell and made my way up to the second floor to check in, only to find I had to share a room with the owner's son. But, at such a late hour, I didn't mind a bit, as I was in no frame of mind to go searching for other accommodations. Following a very needed hot shower, I walked up to the Thorn Tree Café for a cold Tusker beer, and to see who might still be around. As I crossed Kisangi

Boulevard, my eye caught sight of something most unexpected. It was Joe and his overland group getting out of their Land Rover. We shook hands and asked the usual questions of how things were going and what had we been up to since the last time we had seen each other? Joe said his group would be leaving in the morning for the Sudan, having just purchased a couple of cases of beer, in lieu of the required transit permits. Once again, I wished them good luck with the border guards. Then I told Joe, I would be flying to London in two days' time. Later that evening, I walked back to the lodge to catch some much-needed rest that I had missed the night before with the scorpions and bats Also, the beers helped to make up for the "Isiolo Express" adventure!

CHAPTER TEN

March 11, 1975
Nairobi

"*Last day in Africa*" Refreshed from a night's sleep in a bed for the first time in more than a week, I was greeted by the little old man who always brought breakfast to the room. He recognized me right away and nodded to me with a big smile. After breakfast, I ran into Bill who had taken over Ray's old room. Apparently, he was still in financial limbo, not yet having received his money from New York. He had been staying at the Hill Station Lodge for over 3 weeks and had not been asked to pay a cent yet. The people who ran the lodge were very kind and understanding, for sure. Bill and I walked up to the New Stanley Hotel for morning coffee, and I shared my adventures of the past 10 days. Then I hurried to the Post Office to pick up mail, hoping for a letter from Marion. What a joy it was to see her familiar handwriting on the envelope addressed to me. As I read her letter, her tender thoughts filled my heart with joy, and I was even more certain than ever why I was leaving for London the next day. I dashed off a short telegram to let her know my flight arrival information and how much I looked forward to our reunion.

Then I went to the Kenya Coffee House, and as I read her letter again, my thoughts turned to my anticipated arrival in London—how she would meet me and what she would look like now. Many lovely visions filled my head as the time passed. I spent the afternoon revisiting places in Nairobi that had become favorites over the past three months. For me, Nairobi was a beautiful city that I had come to know and appreciate very much, and I knew I would be sad to leave it. There was a final visit to the Danish Pastry Shop for one last pastry, coffee at the Thorn Tree Café for old time's sake, a gin tonic at the Hilton (just because it was the Hilton), and a special treat of the best steak at the "Steak House Restaurant", served with their signature light garlic sauce. It was by far, the best steak I had ever eaten anywhere! I rounded out my last evening in Nairobi with an espresso at the "Milkland Ice Bar", a favorite "drive-in" and teenage hangout in town. Slowly I walked past the New Stanley Hotel for the last time, and then down the narrow, winding streets of the Indian Quarter, past shuttered shops, to my room at the Hill Station Lodge.

Having arrived late in the evening, I found my stuff had been moved to a different room to share with two other guys. As I entered the new room, I recognized a friend from the days on Lamu Island sitting on one of the beds—it was Charles. We talked for a while as I packed my bag in preparation for an early departure in the morning. As we talked, he told me he would be off to India in a few days, aboard the very same ship as John had taken a few weeks earlier. I said I would be off to London tomorrow—how time had passed for both of us. Then we settled in for a night's rest, hoping to avoid being subjected to the barking of the guard dog in the middle of the night, which was always a possibility. Luckily, the people who owned the store below had allowed the dog to be inside, so we were spared the barking. Instead, shortly after we turned out the lights, we became the uninvited guests of an obnoxious, vicious, and horribly loud argument between two whores and a man in the hallway outside our door! It went on and on until we thought it would never end.

Then, just as I was about to storm out the door, a young black girl flung open the door, flicked on the light, and asked stupidly if they had disturbed us! Hell no, of course not—we were just enthralled by it all, and please, would they be kind enough to carry on, as naturally, we hadn't had enough of it yet! I could hardly find enough words to hurl at her fast enough. She quickly ran away and the night returned to peace and quiet—thankfully. I wasn't long before pleasant dreams of Marion filled my head, and I looked forward to our reunion in England, less than 24 hours away.

March 12, 1975
Nairobi, Kenya - London, England

"Now Boarding for London" I was up at dawn the next morning and began the day with a refreshing hot shower. Then, after a quick breakfast, and a fond farewell to the little old man, I hauled my bag across town to the East African Airways City Terminal to catch the shuttle bus to Jomo Kenyatta International Airport. Suddenly, I noticed a large group of people eagerly buying the morning edition of the "Standard" newspaper and talking with everyone about something important. I wondered, "what was of such great interest at the early hour"? I checked my bag at the terminal for the charter flight to London, and then bought a copy of the newspaper. In large, bold black letters on the front page was the headline about the assassination of a prominent government opposition leader! It was very disturbing news for many Kenyans because it was traced back to President Kenyatta's suppression of opposing voices in the government, and the news only served to fan the fires of division among the tribes that made up the nation of Kenya. After reading the news, my thoughts went back several weeks earlier to when John and I were told by a member of the dominant Kikuyu tribe (Kenyatta's tribe), rather matter of factly, that there would be bloodshed when Kenyatta died, and that the Kikuyu would remain on top! It looked like a step in that direction had been taken this day!

But soon, my thoughts turned to the only important thing in the world to me at that moment, my flight to London and my reunion with Marion. Thoughts of our reunion engulfed me as I rode the shuttle bus to the airport, leaving behind the lazy, easy pace of Africa I had known for so many months. As I arrived at the airport, memories of our last hours together as I saw Marion off on her flight to London six weeks earlier came flooding back to my mind. At the time of her departure, I had no idea when I would see her again, or what I would do after she left. The only thing I had known for certain at that time was that we would be together again sometime in the future. But, at the time, I knew not when or where. Now I was embarking on a flight to rejoin her and I was thrilled beyond belief! I bought some Kenyan coffee and two red carnations in the airport before I walked up the steps to board the East African Airways plane. As I settled into my seat, my feelings were torn between how much I would miss Africa and how much more I would miss Marion if I remained any longer.

The flight was a pleasant one, though quite long, more than 8 hours. I occupied myself with many fond memories of my time in Africa, a world over which I was now soaring high above. As the experiences of the past seven months flashed before me, I found myself thinking of my return to Africa someday—for certainly, a piece of me had been left behind there. (several years later, I returned to Africa many times on business and holiday) Finally, as the plane neared England, so did my thoughts focus on Marion. About a half hour from landing in London, as the plane began its slow, deliberate descent, a sudden fear of meeting her again took hold of me! What if all her excited anticipation to see me again was just a figment of my imagination! What if she didn't want me to stay? What if … Hell, why should I have even considered such ridiculous questions! I knew for certain why I was on the plane. Then, all of sudden, and all too fast, after such a long suspension in the air, we were on the ground, surrounded by a million bright lights, darkness, rain, fog, and cold air. It sure wasn't Africa!

I went through Immigration rather mechanically and then rushed to pick up my bag, suddenly aware of a faster pace of life already. Anxiously I searched the incoming luggage for my familiar green rucksack, but it was nowhere to be seen. Other passengers on the flight continued to collect their luggage and rush through Customs, but I could only stand like a deaf mute in search of a sound—my own! Eventually, there were only a handful of us left standing in front of the slowly rotating luggage belt, upon which there were a scattering of unclaimed bags, none that any of us wanted. A sinking feeling came over me as I thought of possibly having lost my entire collection of worldly possessions that I had managed to keep together for over seven months travelling across Africa! Finally, an airline hostess came over to announce the inevitable news we all expected. Some luggage had been left in Nairobi because of overweight limitations. (many of the Indian families had brought everything but the kitchen sink with them) Anxiously, we all checked our luggage tags with her list, but my bag was not among those on the list—so where was my bag?

At that point, I was even more frustrated and pissed off with the airline, the crowd, and everything in general. Then, out of the blue, or more specifically, out of the baggage truck, came a familiar and most welcome sight—my big green rucksack, which I grabbed immediately, lest anyone else try to claim it. Quickly I moved through the "Nothing to Declare" customs lane. Obviously, I had nothing of ordinary value to declare, after all, how would I declare the value of a lifetime's worth of invaluable and irreplaceable experiences and memories from a far-off land? As I exited customs and walked through the doorway into the huge arrivals hall, I suddenly stood facing a sea of strange people, all pale and wide-eyed, each one peering beyond me to others exiting the opaque door. My head twisted back and forth, my eyes in a constant state of motion, my neck straining, desperately trying to see beyond the crowd for the one face I had been longing to see for many weeks.

Haltingly, I walked past the crowd toward the end of the passageway, fearing that perhaps she had not waited for me during the long delay. As I neared the end of the line, a small, smiling figure burst forth and hugged me with a grip twice her own strength. I nearly dropped my rucksack as I strained to respond. Nothing occupied my thoughts at that moment other than the warm sensation of touching the one I loved most of all. The crowd vanished for a few moments and we were only in the present—and together again! I was now holding my future in my arms and Africa was now my past. Then, the reality hit us as we stood outside the terminal building in the cold rain and darkness of the English night. We decided to take a shuttle bus to one of the airport hotels, where we spent our first night together outside Africa. We enjoyed a beautiful night of lovemaking and fell asleep in each other's arms.

March 13, 1975
London, England

"Together Again" The next morning dawned cold and wet, something I wasn't used to after seven months in Africa. We took the train to the London suburb of Richmond where Marion's mother Cathy lived in a small "bedsitter" flat near Kew Gardens. She welcomed me with open arms, and over the course of the next few days, we shared the small one room flat and caught up on the time we had been apart. Eventually, the conversation came around to the question of what we both wanted to do, now that we were together again? After a few days, I rented a room in a small bed and breakfast in the nearby town of Sheen, so as not to impose any longer on Cathy's generous hospitality. Then the next day, out of the blue, I ran into Ray. He was working at a small restaurant in Holland Park, but on the verge of changing jobs. He graciously introduced me to the owner, Mrs Tetther, and the following day I was working as a dishwasher in her restaurant. My shift ran from late afternoon until closing time, which was typically sometime after midnight.

"Tetthers Restaurant" - Holland Park, London

When I first began the job, the chef was from Morocco, but within a week, he had moved on and a Spanish chef took over the kitchen. Jorge and I got along very well—he always had cold beer in the fridge for us and made sure I had plenty of great leftovers to take home at the end of the night. A week or so after I started the dishwashing job, Marion found a job at a shoe shop in Chelsea, so we began looking to rent our own flat. But rents anywhere near Central London were definitely beyond our budget. So, we ended up renting a small two room flat on the edge of Wimbledon. It was a long way from our jobs in London, but it was convenient to bus and tube connections into the city. My routine was six days a week from early afternoon until midnight or later, whereas Marion's job was early morning until late afternoon. Basically, we didn't see much of each other until Sunday, when we both had the day off! Often times, I missed the last train to Wimbledon and had to take the "Late Night Bus" from Earl's Court to the "Tooting Bec Station". Then it was a mile-long walk to reach our flat. Rarely did I see anyone on the street during my late-night walks. But, as summer went on, I would pick a few flowers from people's gardens to leave on the kitchen table for

Marion to find in the morning.

When Sundays came around, we had enough money left over to go out for a pizza and a movie. Even though it was a hard time financially, we shared some very special moments together in our little two room flat on Cromwell Road. As summer moved on, we planted a small garden in the back yard and had some great success with our fruits and veggies. But eventually, the time came when we had to ask ourselves, "what do we want to do"? And the answer was obvious—we wanted to stay together! A short time later, we were married in the County Registrar's Office with Marion's mother Cathy and my Uncle Wally as our witnesses. Earlier I had managed to buy a small silver wedding band in an antique shop on Portobello Road, to make our marriage ceremony official! That evening, back in our small flat, we shared a cake and glass of champagne with Cathy and my Uncle Wally.

Later, Uncle Wally returned to his flat in Wandsworth, and the three of us were about to retire for the night, when suddenly, there was a knock on our front door. As I opened the door, there stood John, toting his old yellow backpack. What a surprise and joy it was to see him again after so many weeks. He had brought us a gift that he had carried all the way from Afghanistan—a gorgeous handcrafted brass tea table! Immediately we thought it was a wedding gift, but lo and behold, John had no idea he had arrived on our wedding day! After more cake and champagne, the four of us finally retired for the night—Marion and I to our single bed in the corner of the sitting room, Cathy to a foam mattress on the kitchen floor, and John to his sleeping bag in the other corner of the sitting room. It certainly wasn't the most private wedding night, but it was a most memorable one!

CHAPTER ELEVEN

"*Starting A New Life Together*" Having taken the big step into marriage, our focus turned to getting an American visa for Marion, that would enable us to travel to the States and start a new life together.

But there was one major hurdle to cross in the visa process, the need for a certified copy of Marion's South African birth certificate, which had to come from Johannesburg. The days of waiting for its arrival were agonizing, but at last, the day came when the postman handed the envelope to Marion and we dashed off to the American embassy to begin the process. Following a rather intensive interview, her visa and green card were issued. That same day, I exchanged my Icelandic Airlines return ticket for two cheap tickets on a charter flight from Brussels to New York. Two days later, we both gave our notice at work and made plans to spend the next few days visiting Marion's mother at her new Victorian flat on the south coast in Brighton, and her father at his lovely old stone cottage in the hills of Shropshire.

Marion's father's cottage in Shropshire, England

Following the lovely late summer visits with Marion's parents, it was time to pack up all our worldly belongings and take the train from London to Brussels. There we boarded the flight to New York. Late in the evening, we arrived in New York and took a shuttle van to an inexpensive motel near JFK airport. The check in process at the motel was a bit scary for both of us, but especially so for Marion, who was seeing policemen carrying guns and a front desk clerk sitting behind a metal screen and bullet-proof glass for the first time in her life! (looking back on that moment, I'm sure she must have questioned the wisdom of immigrating to America) But, the next day we took a train from JFK to Grand Central Terminal in Manhattan, and then another train to Scarsdale to visit with old family friends of Marion who had insisted that we stay with them for a few days. What a totally different world it was from the cheap motel at JFK! Rolf and Vickie made us feel so welcome, like honored guests, as we relaxed by the pool in their lovely garden, accompanied by beautiful Indian Summer weather as well.

Marion in Rolf & Vickie's garden - Scarsdale, NY

On our last evening, Rolf and Vickie treated us to a fabulous dinner at "Sardi's" in lower Manhattan—a truly decadent dining experience for both of us.

The next day, we boarded a flight from La Guardia airport to Orlando, Florida to spend some time with my parents at their retirement home in the small town of Hernando, near Inverness in central Florida. Marion and my mother bonded instantly, both being English, and over the next few days they found so much in common to share.

Marion and me in Florida

The time passed all too quickly, and we had to make plans to travel to Seattle, where I had left a large part of my life over a year before to travel around the world. Being her first time in America, Marion expressed a strong interest in "seeing the country". So, my parents bought us two tickets on the Greyhound bus from Tampa, Florida to Seattle, Washington, a journey that would take four days and a total of more than 2500 miles! It was sad to leave my parents, but a strong bond had been established with Marion, and we were destined to visit them several times later. The first leg of our cross-country adventure was an overnight trip to New Orleans, Houston, and Fort Worth, where we spent a day with my sister.

Then it was another 36 hours to Oklahoma City, Denver, and Cheyenne. Upon arriving in Cheyenne, Wyoming, both of us were exhausted, and the prospect of another sleepless night on the bus was a bit too much to endure. So, we found a nice hotel in Cheyenne and spent a restful night, after having enjoyed a traditional American steak dinner in a classic "cowboy bar" downtown. The next morning, we boarded the bus again for the final leg of our journey that took us to Billings, Great Falls, and Spokane before finally ending our cross-country adventure in Seattle. My old roommates in the communal house near the University of Washington welcomed us with open arms and a whole host of questions about our adventures in Africa, as we sat in front of the fireplace with cups of hot tea. They had even kept my old room downstairs vacant and waiting for my return!

A couple of weeks later, Marion and I found a lovely apartment in an historical building on Capitol Hill, across the street from Volunteer Park. With neither of us having a job, and my savings almost depleted, we had to depend on food stamps for a couple of months. Then, I was offered a job on a research project at the University of Washington, and soon after, Marion was able to find work as a waitress at the "Mouse Trap", a small café in Pioneer Square downtown. At last, we felt like we had a real future together in Seattle.

"North to Alaska" We enjoyed three years in Seattle and made many friends that would continue to be an important part of our life as time went on. Then, I was offered a full-time position with the U.S. Fish and Wildlife Service in Anchorage, Alaska. Before we knew it, the moving van arrived to pick up our stuff, what little furniture we had managed to find at the Salvation Army Thrift Store in Seattle. Suddenly, as spring was in full bloom, we were on our way to Alaska! We decided to drive through Banff and Jasper National Parks in Canada on our way to meet the Alaska ferry in Prince Rupert, BC. My old VW van took us past many spectacular sights, as we travelled with our two little kittens, Jasmine and Chloe, as well as several houseplants. Space in the small van was at a premium, but we made do as best we could. The kittens were constantly on alert as we encountered new and strange sights. A couple of days later, we arrived in Prince Rupert and boarded the Alaska Marine Highway ferry bound for Haines, Alaska, at the

northernmost point of the "Inside Passage". We had a small stateroom on board the ferry, but the kittens had to remain in the van on the car deck below. The 60-hour voyage through the Inside Passage was spectacular, and a very fitting introduction to Alaska.

After arriving in Haines, we began the two-day journey on the Alaska Highway to Anchorage. The route took us through the remote wilderness of the Yukon Territory, a spectacular region of rugged mountains, massive glaciers, rushing rivers, huge lakes, and brilliant forested landscapes. The highway was unpaved from the British Columbia border to the border with Alaska, a distance of more than 300 miles.

On the Alaska Highway – Yukon Territory, Canada

We made an overnight stop in Beaver Creek, Yukon Territory—the westernmost settlement in Canada. Late the next day, we arrived in Anchorage and shared a duplex with our dear friends from Seattle, Bob and Leslie. The trip to Alaska was definitely one of a lifetime! In Anchorage, I worked at the US Fish and Wildlife Service headquarters on a huge project to develop land use plans and environmental impact statements for 80 million acres of new wildlife refuges in Alaska. Marion worked in one of the most popular restaurants in Anchorage, eventually becoming a general manager for the company.

Seven years later, I moved to Vancouver, BC to pursue a PHD program in satellite image analysis at the University of British Columbia. After my studies in Vancouver, I was offered a job in southern California with the world's leading computer mapping company. There, I started out as a software trainer, and ended up managing the annual international users conference as well, that was attended by 15,000 people from more than 120 countries around the world. During my 25 years as a software trainer, I had the good fortune to travel to more than 80 countries teaching classes, and even to visit some of the places I had been on the overland journey 30 years earlier. That pretty much brings my story up to date. But many things have changed in Africa since my journey, and it would be virtually impossible now to repeat the same trip as in 1974-75!

EPILOGUE

"*And What About Now?*" Naturally, during the years since the overland journey, the situation in Africa had changed dramatically, mostly for the worse. To try and repeat my overland trip across Africa would be impossible today, given the political unrest, travel restrictions, civil war, genocide, and epidemics, like the devastating outbreaks of the Ebola virus. (reflecting upon the good fortune I had to be able to travel in Africa when I did, I was so lucky to be in the right places at the right times!)

That pretty much brings my life up to date. I am semi-retired and enjoying my passion for travel, photography, and writing. The future looks very bright and one that I continue to look forward to.

On a post-note, my dear friend and traveling companion John, passed away many years ago now, while he was riding a horse on a beach in Morocco. The news of his death from his sister made me feel very sad. But I also knew he had died doing what he loved the most —traveling the world, searching out new experiences, meeting interesting people in strange far-off lands, and living among different cultures. He was the consummate world traveler, and I feel so fortunate and privileged to have been able to share a part of his remarkable life! I will forever keep fond memories of him in my heart —rest in peace John!

And one day, two years ago, I received the news of Stuart's death from his longtime companion, the result of a massive heart attack he suffered while driving on his game reserve in South Africa. His passing was an emotional moment for me. He and I had been through so much together on the journey across Africa—he was like a brother to me!

So, I dedicate this book to the memory of John and Stuart—may they both rest in peace!

APPENDIX/ADDENDUM

Travels with King Kong

Miles / Kilometers traveled:	Miles	Kilometers
Tangier, Morocco – Fez, Morocco	190	305
Fez, Morocco – Marrakech, Morocco	308	496
Marrakech, Morocco – Figuig, Morocco	541	871
Figuig, Morocco – Ain Salah, Algeria	823	1325
Ain Salah, Algeria – Tamanrasset, Algeria	412	664
Tamanrasset, Algeria – In Guezzem, Algeria	241	389
In Guezzem, Algeria – Arlit, Niger	150	241
Arlit, Niger – Zinder, Niger	425	685
Zinder, Niger – Kano, Nigeria	170	275
Kano, Nigeria – Maiduguri, Nigeria	367	592
Maiduguri, Nigeria – Bangui, CAR	956	1539
Bangui, CAR – Mobaye, Zaire	372	600
Mobaye, Zaire – Yakoma, Zaire	93	150
Yakoma, Zaire – Basoko, Zaire	326	525
Basoko, Zaire – Kisangani, Zaire	168	271
Kisangani, Zaire – Komanda, Zaire	390	628
Komanda, Zaire – Goma, Zaire	303	488
Goma, Zaire – Kigali, Rwanda	105	169
Kigali, Rwanda – Mwanza, Tanzania	335	540
Mwanza, Tanzania – Arusha, Tanzania	385	621

Arusha, Tanzania – Amboseli NP, Kenya	114	185
Amboseli NP, Kenya – Nairobi, Kenya	150	242
	7,332	11,800

September 12, 1974–January 2, 1975 (112 days)

Average per day: 65 miles / 105 kilometers

www.ingramcontent.com/pod-product-compliance
Lightning Source LLC
Chambersburg PA
CBHW071147130626
46553CB00004B/1558